I DIDN'T REALLY KNOW HIM
Married to an Englishman

by

Fauneil Fremont

i

ISBN: 978-1-965951-32-3 (sc)

Seraphim Global Media LLC
155 Willowbrook Blvd Ste 110 Wayne, NJ 07470
+1 888-347-1877
fullfillment@seraphimgml.com

CHAPTERS

Introduction

To the Reader from the Author:

My late husband's poems, autobiographical sketches, and quotes from his father's memoirs are verbatim. Also, all historical facts, place names, and time periods are non-fiction. The names of all characters and incidental names are fictional.

Chapter I:The Meeting

I, Beth, married an Englishman named Will, at a time when life when simpler than it is today. Until I was in the fifth grade, my parents and we three girls, Nancy, Elizabeth (Beth), and Amy, had lived in Hoskins, a very small rural village in northeastern Nebraska. It was the same community where my grandparents and my great grandparents had lived after they had emigrated from Germany. I grew up with their stories of the hardship of life on a prairie, drought, and The Great Depression. My ancestors had been rugged, hard-working, goal-centered people who had a belief in God and a strong desire to make life better for the next generation.

My sister, Nancy, and I, being only fifteen months apart in age, were best "buddies" as we wandered about Hoskins during our childhood. When Mom was taking Dad's place at the rural bank during his hail-adjusting trips, we were looked after by Agatha, a middle-aged spinster. Doting on baby Amy, she allowed us older girls to leave the house for unsupervised times. We wandered about the village, sneaking into an old, abandoned hotel, stopping by to say "Hi" to the postmistress, and going into the schoolyard to get water from the outdoor pump to make mud for our bee stings. Near home, we picked wild grapes growing alongside the road, looked for crawdads in a nearby stream, and discussed how to rescue a rabbit that had fallen into a dry well. Nancy, the "big sister," was always protective of me. As we roamed, she warned me about poison oak or a rut-hole in the dirt road.

Raising us during The Great Depression was a struggle for our parents. Married in 1932, they had worked hard to provide food and shelter for their family. Mom remade clothes for us from hand-me-downs given to her by a neighbor lady. She baked bread each day; she canned meat, fruits, and vegetables that Grandmother had brought in from her farm; she kept a clean house even though the only running water available was from the kitchen pump.

Dad, too, was very hardworking but humble enough to accept any work that could help his family. One winter season when the snow was blocking the businesses all over town, Dad scooped snow from morning until night, making a total of thirty cents a day, enough to buy flour for bread. Before moving into town, he had tried farming on Grandmother's land, but a relentless drought had forced him back to town. Next, he opened a small grocery store, hoping to make a small profit primarily from farmers. They came into town on the weekends to sell their chickens, eggs, milk, and cream. Dad gave them credit for each item and then allowed them to purchase fruits, vegetables, and staples from the store.

When the depression began to lift, the bank reopened, and farmers needed crop adjustors to evaluate their losses after it hailed. Next, Dad started an insurance and real estate business. When World War II began, the economy began booming. Dad and Mom moved our family to the larger town of Norfolk, fifteen miles away from Hoskins. They wanted us three girls to have more advantages in education and music and Dad to have more opportunities in business.

Except for the first year of adjusting to a new community, I was a happy child and teenager, excelling in school and piano performance. I earned a scholarship to the University of Nebraska. Upon graduating in 1956, I joined a study group for a summer trip to Europe, borrowing the money from my father, which I repaid during my first year of teaching English in Tucson, Arizona. While teaching I attended the University of Arizona as a student at night. During the summers, I became a full-time student until I earned my M.Ed. degree in 1959. During my final summer at the U of A, I met Frank, who was finishing an MBA degree. We fell in love and were engaged by the end of the summer.

Frank and I wanted to start our careers in San Jose, California. I found a teaching job in a high school, and he became a realtor. Though engaged, we did not live together before marriage. (In 1959, many girls tried to follow the adage, "First the engagement, then the marriage, then the baby carriage.") However, the engagement didn't work out, and by January of 1959, I began to think that I would end up an "old maid" school teacher, like my mother's aunt had unhappily called herself.

*   *   *

In February of 1960 Will, a charming and witty Englishman, and I met at the swimming pool of the apartment complex where we both lived. I was swimming, and Will was playing bridge by the side of the pool. When the fourth player left, Will asked me to join them. I was wearing a baby blue, one-piece bathing suit with tiny buttons in front. I could tell from his look that he found my figure attractive.

Although Will found me attractive, we became only casual friends for the next six months. Will had a girlfriend named Mary in Los Angeles, and I was occasionally dating Bill, a young man who traveled between San Jose and

Tucson. From the beginning, I was unsure about Will's intentions towards me. We lived only a few yards apart at the apartment, but we never spent personal time together. Instead, he called me almost daily for long chats on the telephone. He seemed to want to talk about Mary and to encourage me to talk about Bill. Since I did not want to discuss Bill with him, I usually managed to encourage him to tell me about his background.

Chapter II: Getting to Know You

Will liked to talk about himself, and within the next two weeks I learned everything about him that he wanted me to know. He had grown up in Peterborough, England, where one of the old Norman cathedrals dominated the town and its central square. His mother Laura and his father Clyde were bookkeepers, she in a florist's shop and he in a brick company.

His mother was the oldest in a family of eight girls, and Will became the first male born in the family for years. He had been christened with an important-sounding name, William Parker Hayes, worthy of his place in the family. He had been the favorite grandchild of his grandfather, a prominent detective in the Peterborough police. Through his grandfather and his parents, Will had received the best schooling available in the area at the Deacon's School for Boys.

At age nine, when Will became dangerously ill with encephalitis and rheumatic fever, his parents provided him with private medical treatment and nursing care for six months. The doctors warned his parents that Will's heart had been damaged, and when he finally returned to school, he was not allowed to play sports. Also, he was not promoted to the next grade level because his mother insisted that he repeat the year.

In spite of being held back a year, he was ready for the university at age seventeen. He wanted to go to Cambridge, but his mother wanted him to stay near her so that she could watch over him. He applied to and was accepted by the outlying branch of the University of London, which was a day's bicycle ride from Peterborough.

At the university, Will studied pure math and physics and was in the top group of ten students during his first year. Will worked diligently during his first year. He was determined to succeed. However, a physics professor was worried about Will's intensity and suggested that Will take up a hobby for relaxation.

Will started fencing and playing bridge, which became an addiction. He played bridge with fellow students hour after hour, often skipping professors' lectures or failing to study. He felt, like George Bernard Shaw, that bridge was "the most entertaining and intelligent game the wit of man" has invented. Therefore, two years later, when he graduated with a third-class degree instead of a first-class one, he was not surprised. However, he blamed his physics professor for removing him from the top group of ten students.

Upon graduating, Will was hired as an aeronautical engineering trainee at Vickers Super Marine, an airplane company in Southampton, England, the distance of a fairly short train trip from Peterborough. He remained there for three years. I learned that he had been in Southampton when my ship docked there in the summer of 1956, and we could have met at that time if our paths had crossed.

By the end of that summer, Will had decided to emigrate to Toronto, Canada for a better paying position as a stress engineer at Avro Aircraft. In Toronto he moved into a house with four other bachelor roommates. They were intelligent, young men who shared his interests in bridge, reading, writing, traveling, and classical music. Will auditioned for and became a member of the famous Toronto Mendelssohn Choir. In England he had studied voice and violin and was well-trained for the performances the choir gave.

In 1959, Will emigrated to the U.S, taking work in temporary job-shop situations to allow himself more freedom to go skiing. After a year of this, he moved to L.A., where he was trained in computers by I.B.M., who then sent him to their branch in San Jose. It took Will ten years to become completely independent, but little by little, he had achieved it.

* * *

During the three years that Will lived in Canada, his friend Barry saw Will as quite a ladies' man. When Will was leaving Avro Aircraft, Barry presented him with a farewell poem:

> *Farewell, my Will – Fate indeed is cruel*
> *To prise from Avro's Crown so fair a Jewel,*
> *A Gem of many facets, polished fair –*
> *Oh! never did we see a bird so rare.*
> *Stress, Music, Aerodynamics, Maths,*
> *Surefooted he on all these divers' paths;*
> *Poetry, too. Surely if his endeavor*
> *Was centred on one Goal, I should think never*
> *Were Laurels quite so handy to be clutched.*
> *Why, many have I heard say, "Is he touched*
> *by Genius?" Ah! fortunate my way*
> *To work with such a colleague day by day.*
>
> *Have patience with me, friends, do not bewail*
> *If I am prolix; truly I would fail*
> *To do him justice if I did not mention*

His way with ladies. Never, do I think
Has man stepped so surefooted on the brink
of Matrimony. And yet when romance ends
The lady counts him still amongst her friends.
He always seems sincere upon his part –
He is a Cunning Dog, he knows the Art
Of Love from Ovid via Marie Stopes,
Clean through to Kinsey – yes – he knows the ropes
To woo so many, yet stay clear of Marriage.
Yet mark you this, I mean not to disparage
His Honour or intentions, - 'tis not done,
And much that I have said is said in fun.
But truly now – we hate to see you leave
And if we do not seem to deeply grieve
Your leaving us is not so sweet a sorrow –
Let's hope for your return some fair to-morrow.

(Note: The spelling of the words is Canadian.)
January, 1959, Toronto

*   *   *

Barry described Will's "genius," his diverse talents, and his ability to stay clear of marriage. When Will left Canada for Colorado, he was not looking to further his career, but for pleasure on the skiing slopes. He was ready to relax and enjoy life while he was still young. Rather than a permanent job in aerodynamics, he took temporary job-shop positions, making just enough money to pay for his skiing expenses. In order to enjoy the popular slopes in Colorado, he moved from Denver to Aurora to Colorado Springs. When the skiing season ended, he sought permanent employment in the aero industry, but he couldn't get a security clearance. At this point, he had to change his career, and so he moved to California where I.B.M. was hiring computer trainees.

On I.B.M.'s entrance exam, Will scored the highest of any of their trainees at that time. He had a promising career ahead of him. However, when the winter season began, Will headed for the nearby ski slopes during the weekends. On Mondays following a ski trip, he was exhausted from the activity. His manager reported that it took Will three days to perform well at work because he was so tired. Not wanting to lose the promise that Will had first shown, I.B.M. moved him to San Jose, California in February of 1960.

The move meant not only a change in location, but a change in female companionship. After Will left England, he pursued his passions, and he began writing love poems. He seemed to fall in love every month with a different girl, writing to and wooing Gisela in January, Joan in February, Jane in March, Carol in April and May, Joan again in July, Janice in August. In his June poem (no name given), he summed up his passion:

> *My love is like a flaming fire,*
> *That feeds the flames of my desire,*
> *And burns upon the funeral pyre*
> *Of my lost bachelorhood.*
>
>   *   *   *

Many of the young women were part of the weekend skiing crowds, which Will described as "a way of life unto itself":

> *What is skiing?*
> *To ski is to fly like a bird, to ski*

Is to encounter speed in the raw, to ski
Is to begin to live dangerously and to revel
In near brushes with disaster. Skiing is
A special kind of individual physical freedom,
A new way of escaping from the stresses of life
And the best way to fill your lungs with
Vitalizing mountain air. And of the camaraderie
Of skiers who can write. Of the pale beer,
The dark beer, the bawdy songs, the libido
And its fulfilment in a way not wanton,
But with the shared satisfaction of healthy sex.
To ski is a way of life unto itself.

* * *

When Will left L.A., he left behind his girlfriend, Mary, who was a colleague at work. He considered her highly intelligent and serious, unlike the "skiing gals." As he kept in touch with her after the move, his letters became increasingly amorous, indicating that he was beginning to consider a long-term relationship. However, instead of flying to L.A. to visit Mary on a weekend, he drove to the ski slopes of the Sierra Nevada Mountains, which were only five hours away from San Jose.

Towards the end of March, the snow in the mountains began to melt, ending the skiing season. During the first weekend following the closure of Heavenly Valley, Will called me. He had received a "Dear John" letter from Mary. She had started dating another trainee at I.B.M. Will was distraught; he had made plans to fly to L.A. for a surprise visit to Mary. He read to me the poem that he had written, which he planned to give to Mary:

I need you, how I need you,

And we're many miles apart.
I want to kiss you and hold you,
Caressingly enfold you –
I never yet have told you
That we must never part.
O let me hold you,
Let me embrace you,
Kissing away all your cares and fears;
Lovingly tend you
And tenderly love you,
Whispering love's message so softly in your ears.

*   *   *

During April, Will and I talked only on the phone. Much of our conversation was still about Mary. In May and June, we began to spend time with each other as friends. Will invited me to be a fourth for a game of bridge at the swimming pool or with two co-workers at the I.B.M. plant on the weekend. We also began to play music together, he on the violin, I on the piano. I had borrowed a set of keys to the high school from an administrator, and we sometimes went there on a Saturday to use the piano in the music room. Having graduated from the Catholic Conservatory of Music in Norfolk when I was fifteen, I was skilled in classical music. Will had been the first chair violinist in the youth orchestra in Peterborough.

In July, our encounters were upgraded from a friendship to a beginning romance. We had evening walks together, watched movies, and enjoyed lunches or inexpensive dinners at home or in the neighborhood. We expanded our chats to include books, plays, musicals, painting, photography, travel, religion, and former experiences in places we had lived or worked.

Will seemed to enjoy my companionship, and I was beginning to find his English accent, his vocabulary, and his English ways appealing. He was a welcome change from the American young men I had dated. Aside from skiing, he was not interested in sports or in bodybuilding. He did not often look at himself in the mirror.

*   *   *

At the beginning of August, Will was given a bad performance review at work and then fired. This was a wake-up call for him. He had no income; he had accumulated much debt from the expensive sport of skiing, and his parents were arriving from England in two weeks. Also, he had a fear of being deported as an unemployed non-citizen. What could he do? How could he appear to his parents as the serious young man of promise they thought him to be? He could not tell them that he had been fired. He knew that his mother would take the opportunity to encourage him to return to England and to settle down with a pretty English girl.

His solution to the problem was to involve me in the ploy that we were on the verge of engagement. To distract from not going to work, he would pretend to be on vacation so that he could take his parents by car on a long sightseeing tour.

I agreed to the "engagement" ploy. In fact, I helped him to clean his messy apartment before his parents arrived. First, I tackled all of the clutter left on counters and floors. I encouraged him to purchase a bookcase to display his books that were lying about. I stored the National Geographic magazines in his closet and threw the rest of the magazines in the trash, along with old newspapers and junk mail. Then I turned my attention to the bedroom and bath.

I laundered the sheets, cleaned the fixtures and the shower in the bathroom, and stored his medicines and personal items in the cabinet above the sink. After thoroughly washing down the kitchen counters, cupboards, and floors, and cleaning the oven, stove, and refrigerator, I began cleaning the living room: dusting the furniture and vacuuming the upholstery and the carpet.

The apartment, which was on the first floor, had a small enclosed garden, which was full of weeds. I encouraged Will to pull the weeds and replace them with plantings of star jasmine, zinnias, asters, and alyssum. After we had finished our work, we walked to the local pizza parlor for pizza and beer. As we clinked our mugs, Will said, "To you, Beth. You have all of the qualities needed in a 'good little housewife.'"

Shortly after his parents arrived, I showed them American hospitality by inviting them to dinner. I prepared a meal that I knew the English always enjoyed: roast beef with Yorkshire pudding, roasted potatoes and carrots, and trifle for dessert.

After dinner, Will took his father Clyde for a walk. Will later reported to me that his father had been very impressed with me and had said, "If you don't marry that girl, you're a damned fool." Will convinced his father that we were well on our way to a lasting relationship; we had been dating since February; we had been playing violin and piano together. We had good-paying jobs; we were ready for an engagement.

While Clyde and Will were walking, Laura was helping me with the dishes in the kitchen. This was Laura's opportunity to "talk my ears off." She started by telling me that she was the oldest of eight girls. Her father had been a prominent detective in the police force, and her mother had "upper class" blood in her veins, hence Will's name, William Parker Hayes. 'Parker' is a family name, which otherwise would have been lost since there were no boys in the family.

"I wondered about the name 'Parker,' I commented.

"Of course," she answered. Laura continued by talking about her marriage with Clyde. They had met when they had lead roles in a musical production in Peterborough. At the time, they were both bookkeepers, Clyde at a brick-making company, and Laura in a florist shop. In 1930, they were married, and Will was born in 1932. Laura and two of her sisters contracted scarlet fever during her pregnancy. Her sisters died, and Laura's baby, Will, was born with a mild heart defect. World War II started when Will was six years old. The country was in turmoil during most of Will's school years. "When he was nine, he came down with encephalitis and rheumatic fever," Laura added.

"Will told me a little about that time," Beth remarked.

"It was a miracle that he survived," Laura continued. "Will was left with a very bad heart murmur. The doctor warned Clyde and me that he might not reach age ten." I did not respond. I was thinking about Will's skiing weekends and the stamina the sport demanded. The door opened. Clyde and Will had returned. Before the evening ended, Will showed his parents a map of the U. S., on which he had highlighted the travel route he planned for them. The car trip would take them to Yosemite and Zion Parks, the Grand Canyon, L.A. and north on Highway One through Carmel and Monterey. Finally, he planned to drive them across the

U.S. to New York City, where they would board the Queen Elizabeth for an ocean trip back to England.

Will was traveling with his parents for the remainder of August and into September. Immediately upon his return to San Jose, he found work as a mathematician at Food Machinery Corporation (FMC). Shortly after acquiring his position, Will began to view me as a possible marriage partner. Because of all of the debt from his month of travel and his skiing expenses, he must have felt that I was a good "catch." I was in my fifth year of teaching, had earned two degrees, and had lived a life of moderation and frugality. My lifestyle was totally unlike that of his former ski amours.

On the Saturday before his 28th birthday, he took me to dinner at The Iron Horse in San Francisco. It was located on Maiden Lane, a narrow "alley" street, not far from Union Square. When we entered, I felt like we were in an English pub connected to a fine restaurant. In the pub, we took seats next to a cheerful fire in the corner fireplace, where we had martinis. The restaurant was a square-shaped room with tables and upholstered benches along the outer edges of the room. Will directed me to a bench so that we could sit closely next to each other. As I looked around, I was reminded of similar English restaurants that I had experienced during my summer study tour of Europe. The walls of the room were paneled in beautiful mahogany wood, the upholstery looked like needlepoint, and lovely stained-glass windows alternated with paintings of English hunting scenes. Will ordered for us a typical fine English meal: leg of lamb, roasted potatoes and vegetable, and a rum trifle for dessert. During our after-dinner coffee and cognac, Will reached into the breast pocket of his suit and handed me a poem:

Will you be girlfriend, oh girl of brown hair,
Or will you waltz past me with nose in the air?
Will you be sweetheart, my lass of fair face,
Or do I plead vainly my love-sick case?
Will you be lover, and lend me your charms,
Or scorning, refuse to lie in my arms?
Will you be promised and accept my ring,
Or will you reject my fond offering?

After I had read it, he took my hand and repeated the question: *Will you?*

"*Yes,* I answered. *"It seems that our engagement ploy turned into reality."*

*   *   *

Chapter III: Marriage and Birth

My parents wanted us to be married in Nebraska. Since I was busy with teaching, and Will could have only two weeks absence from work, I asked my mother to make all of the wedding arrangements for us. She was happy to do that. When Mom and Dad were married in 1932, The Great Depression prohibited them from a church wedding. Now Mom reserved the church, rented the reception hall, ordered the flowers and the wedding cake, sent out invitations, and contacted family members to participate in the ceremony.

All that was left for me to do was to choose the color and fabric of the gowns for my two sisters (I chose green velvet), and to shop for my own gown, which I purchased myself. I went to the expensive I. Magnin Store in San Francisco, where I chose a full-length gown of heavy taffeta, with tiny buttons down the back and lace inserts along the square off-shoulder neckline. The inserts matched the lace of the long veil. Will and his attendants, who were my cousins, would be attired in blue suits rather than tuxedos, to keep down the expense for the family.

Like most grooms in 1960, Will was in charge of the honeymoon. He suggested that we should drive from Norfolk to Aspen, Colorado, where we would ski for a week before motoring back to California. Since I had never skied, I had visions of spending the days alone on the bunny slope while he raced down the slopes. He convinced me that it would not take me long to learn because I had engaged in so many athletic activities. I agreed to try skiing, but when I asked him for information regarding our lodging, he said that he wanted it to be a surprise.

Since I had more vacation time than Will, I drove my car to Nebraska so that we would have transportation for the honeymoon. When Will arrived by plane five days later, we went to the Madison County Courthouse for our marriage licenses. That evening was the rehearsal dinner, which was prepared by my seventy-five-year-old grandmother as a gift to me and the family. She and Will liked each other a lot even though she had trouble understanding his accent.

I remember well our wedding day! It was a beautiful Christmas Day in Nebraska. A light snow was falling, and colorful lights were everywhere. No decorations inside the church were needed – the trees and poinsettias were still there from the morning service. My father thought that I looked beautiful in my gown, but Will only nodded at me when Dad "handed me over to him." To me, Will looked tense and uneasy, but he perked up later at the reception. In the greeting line of the guests, Dad stood next to Will and me. Will spoke enthusiastically to each guest, but Dad had trouble with his accent and kept turning to me for an interpretation.

Following the reception, our immediate family went back to my parents' house, where Mom had ready a buffet supper. We drank wine, ate, and exchanged Christmas gifts before Will and I left for Grand Island, where we would spend our wedding night. Three hours later, by the time we arrived at the hotel, Will was feeling sick. (Throughout our marriage, Will often wrote pithy poems about longing or sickness.) His poem from March, 1960 might have been written on our wedding night:

O where is all the spirit now?

Where is all the cheer?
Where is all the festive cup?
I've spewed it up, I fear.

The next day, sick Will and I were headed by car for Aspen, Colorado, our honeymoon destination. It was a long day's drive, and we were both tired when we got to Aspen. However, I was looking forward to a romantic ambience: a cabin retreat with a fire glowing in a large stone fireplace and flowers and champagne awaiting our arrival.

What a shock I felt as we entered the kitchen of a smelly, tacky fishing cabin: linoleum on the floor, an old stove and refrigerator available, a wall heater instead of a fireplace, and an old narrow double bed, comfortable only for one. I couldn't help blurting out, "If you expect me to cook, you're crazy!" Another night without intimacy followed. Will slept in the narrow bed; I took the battered fake leather couch.

The next day Will was feeling better, and I had decided to not let our poor accommodations ruin our honeymoon. With Will's large amount of debt, the fishing cabin was probably all he could afford. We started anew. Intimacy at night followed day-time fun. A large stone fireplace in the gathering room provided a cheery blaze and a much-needed atmosphere for love. We both enjoyed the camaraderie of other young couples, some who were also honeymooners.

Will was happy that I needed only one day on the bunny slope before I was ready for the intermediate slope. My activities of swimming, tennis, skating and sledding, square dancing, along with my lifestyle of moderation had paid off. By the end of our time in Aspen, I could see why

Will loved skiing so much. It was an invigorating, exciting sport.

*   *   *

Seven weeks later, we took a weekend trip to Squaw Valley to ski for the Lincoln Holiday weekend. We skied a little the first day, but then a blizzard arose, and we became trapped inside our room. There was no television, and we had not bothered to bring books with us. Suddenly with no romantic build-up, Will said, "Let's make a baby."

I was surprised at Will's sudden desire for a baby. We had not yet discussed parenthood. Being newly married and busy as an English teacher, I had not really thought much about motherhood. I wanted to be wooed and romanced and loved for myself. I wanted time to learn to better know the man I had married. However, I succumbed to his emotion, and our baby was conceived.

*   *   *

I was miserable with morning sickness during the remainder of the school term. My body was rapidly changing internally and then finally externally. I wanted to be asked, "Can I get you something?" Or I wanted to be told, "You look beautiful to me" or "I hope the baby has your lovely blue eyes, Beth."

When school ended for the summer and my morning sickness was gone, I began to feel less self-absorbed, and I was full of energy. I turned a bedroom in our new house into a nursery by painting the walls yellow and decorating with items that a newborn would enjoy. A neighbor had given me an old wooden rocking chair that I sanded and painted white. I anticipated using it for rocking, singing, reading, and comforting our baby.

Not long after our adorable Dora was born, my parents came to visit and to see Dora baptized. They stayed for a week, with my mother helping me around the house so that I could recuperate from the birth, and my dad watching me becoming a mother. Before they left, Dad snapped a photo of Will with his arm around me as I held Dora on the front steps of our house – a picture of tender love.

For the next six months, tenderness and loving feelings continued among the three of us. Will wrote two sweet poems at this time, which he shared with me:

*   *   *

The Newcomer

Little wife comes home tomorrow,
Bringin' baby home as well –
Little wife I love so dearly:
Love her more than I can tell.
Now two sweet ones I have love for-
Little wife and babe as well;
Darling wife I love so dearly,
Love her more than I can tell.
'Neath one roof we'll live together,
And our little dog as well.
For our daughter then a brother!
And another 'gal' as well!
In my fam'ly I take pleasure –
In my fam'ly pride as well;
In my wife who loves me dearly,
Pride and pleasure blend so well.

Who's This Little Stranger

Who's this little stranger
that's not a little stranger anymore?
She's the sweetest little baby
that San Jose or California ever saw:
At three months old she smiles and coos
and very nearly talks –
She almost sits, and almost stands
and darned near even walks.

* * *

Fate was unkind. Dreams of a brother and sister for Dora were not to be. When I gave birth to Dora, a part of the after-birth remained imbedded so deeply within the walls of the uterus that the doctor could not remove it although he finally painfully yanked out what he thought was all of it. However, small unseen portions remained. In the ensuring months, it developed into a hydatid mole. My uterus thought it was still feeding a developing fetus, supplying it with continual nourishment and blood. The mole grew so rapidly, I looked like I was carrying twins within a few months. The doctor was convinced that I was pregnant again even though I was nursing Dora.

By the end of May of 1962, Will was sent to Washington D.C. by Control Data Corporation to work on a three-month project. He managed to find a way so that Dora and I could accompany him. We had been in D.C. for only a few weeks before I began to have massive hemorrhages. A doctor at Prince George's Hospital diagnosed my case correctly, and I was taken in for an emergency hysterotomy within a few hours.

My heart was so enlarged from the months of trying to supply blood that the surgeons had to perform the operation with localized anesthesia via needles into the abdomen. As I lay on the operating table, I could not feel my abdomen, but I could hear the surgeons preparing for surgery, swathing the area, cutting open the abdomen and then the uterus. I heard one of them gasp as he removed the mole. I caught a glimpse of a cluster of what looked like white grapes before it fell apart.

I felt my heart pounding violently. Suddenly I couldn't breathe. As I suffered heart failure, my head felt like it was gyrating rapidly back and forth. Then my spirit escaped from my body, and I experienced rapidly being propelled through a long, dark tunnel. Finally, the tunnel ended, and I was alone in the darkness. It seemed like I was in a "no-man's space" with nothing but my own thoughts. At first, my thoughts centered on all of the past, even insignificant words or deeds that I had forgotten but could now remember. After this period of reflection, I felt the loneliness of knowing that I could be here alone for all eternity. The fear of eternal solitude was unbearable, and I cried out, GOD HELP ME!

Immediately an extremely bright, yet warm and comforting light appeared. I felt that the light indicated God's presence. The light and I had an unspoken conversation. Although we communicated about many subjects, I only remember my asking God to return me to earth so that I could care for Dora.

Gradually, I felt my spirit returning to my body. Although frightening, the feeling of being only a spirit had been free and light in comparison with the heaviness of gravity I felt as my spirit reunited with my body. I found myself again struggling for each breath. I did not know that the doctors had restarted my heart on the operating table and had given me an infusion of many pints of blood. When they succeeded in bringing me back to the land of the living, they moved me to intensive care where I was put into an oxygen tent.

Meanwhile, Will had been waiting with anxiety and fear, first at the hospital, and then throughout the coming weeks as I did not recover. He expressed his feelings in his poem called *"Waiting."*

> *Under the Washington sky without you,*
> *Not any pleasure, and no-one to woo,*
> *Easy to see why I married you, dear,*
> *I'm never alone when I have you near.*
> *God gave me you to share the long, still hours,*
> *Sweet scent of pleasure, the perfume of flow'rs.*
> *Now I fear to close my eyes in my gloom;*
> *Listless I wait near the phone in my room.*
> *Hundreds of minutes with nothing to do,*
> *Suffering the pain of waiting for you.*

*   *   *

I was in the hospital in D.C. during June and July while Mother took care of Dora. My sister Donna flew from Nebraska to stay at my bedside. Somehow, she must have known that she would be needed to save me. One afternoon while Will was sitting and reading in my room, Donna was watching closely at my bedside. A nurse came into the room and changed the oxygen canister, but she forgot to turn back on the oxygen machine. Donna watched as my breathing became more and more labored. Finally, she turned to Will and said, "There's something wrong. The little red ball should be jumping up and down, and Beth is breathing her own carbon dioxide." "Don't be silly, Donna," Will responded. "The nurses know what they're doing." Donna ignored him and ran out to the nurses' station, demanding a nurse to come immediately. Will was gracious enough to admit that he had been wrong.

By the end of July, I was able to travel to my parents' home in Nebraska, where further surgeries were performed in the Lutheran Hospital, the last one being a hysterectomy-ovariectomy when the doctor discovered that choreo-carcinoma had developed. Will stayed in Washington until his project had been completed. During this time, he wrote his touching poem, *"The Summer of '62"*:

> *Honey, Honey, - O Beth my sweet Honey,*
> *I'm watching and waiting and praying for you –*
> *Dull ache within me – I'm fighting my fears:*
> *How slim the chance you will live!*
> *As each minute passes, I add thirty more –*
> *Doctor and surgeon arrive looking stern;*
> *It's done! – "though she's not out of danger."*
> *Long hours now, the fam'ly vigil of love:*
> > *Oxygen tent with no oxygen flow!*
> > *Running a fever not once, but ten times,*
> > *Antiseptic shots, pints of blood by the score.*
> *Minutes and hours pass to days and to weeks,*
> *In – out of urgent care many more times –*
> *Leave you I must...to another "white coat."*

End of the summer...but no end to this!

*   *   *

When I was released from the hospital, I was reunited with Dora, who had learned to walk at Mom and Dad's home. At first, she thought I was a stranger. I said to Mom, "She thinks you're her mother now." Mother assured me that Dora would remember me as her mother as soon as I began to take care of her. I started to try to bond with Dora again by taking her for walks in her stroller. It was already fall. A cold snap had occurred, causing the beautiful Nebraska leaves to turn golden and red and to begin to fall. As we walked, the wheels of the baby carriage crunched the leaves. "Listen to the leaves, Dora," I said. "They're saying *Crunch, Crunch.* I remember you."

Chapter IV: Recovery

I finally flew home with Dora to San Jose in mid-September and was placed under the care of doctors there for further treatment and observation. I wish I could remember much that happened during the next four months, but I was too sick to do more than daily survive and care for Dora as best I could.

I only remember vividly one beautiful experience when Dora was about eleven months and was becoming adept at walking. She was in my care. I became extremely tired in the afternoon and badly needed a nap. I fed her, gave her a glass of milk, changed her diaper, gathered up some of her toys, fetched our dog Fritz, and enclosed us in a small guest bedroom, making sure the door was secure. The room was bare except for a carpet on the floor and a hide-a-bed. When Dora was busy with her play, I settled on the couch and fell into a deep sleep. When I awoke hours later, I found that Dora had crawled up onto the couch and had stretched herself across me, nestling her head against my neck. What a precious moment that was for me!

Holes in my memory of the days from September through January were never filled by anything Will wrote at the time or later. I do not know when he went to work or when he came home. Did he take care of meals? Did he do laundry, clean bathrooms, vacuum, feed the dog, care for Dora, entertain himself, or communicate with my parents?

From an entry in his father's memoirs, I gathered that there had been little communication to his parents about the summer and fall of 1962. Clyde wrote, "*Their daughter was born in November. There was to be another addition to the family the next year, but something went wrong, and she was not able to have any more children, so Dora is the one and only."*

By the end of January, 1963, my chemotherapy was over, and I was beginning to feel better and stronger each day. The cancer had been arrested, but it would be five years before it could be termed conquered. I was thankful for each new day. I loved being in our humble little home and taking care of our precious toddler. When spring and then summer arrived, I took Dora for daily walks in the sunshine, accompanied by Fritz.

My bubble of happiness burst at the end of July. Will, like his whimsical character, Tommy Titmouse, informed me that we needed a bigger house:

> *Little Tommy Titmouse*
> *Didn't know what to do –*
> *He had a very tiny house,*
> *Just big enough for two.*
>
> *Then one morning she said,*
> *His little wife, said she,*
> *As she lay snug in bed,*
> *"Tomorrow there'll be three."*
>
> *There was just nothing for it –*
> *If that really was the case –*
> *He'd have to hunt around a bit,*
> *And find a bigger place!*

*   *   *

Will and his mother Laura had been communicating about plans for them to come to California to live with us when Clyde retired in September, 1964. Will did not share the plan with me. Clyde was not the instigator of the plan, but he wrote about it in his memoirs: "*Will suggested that when I reached sixty-five, I should retire from the brick company. He would build a house large enough, so that we could have our own apartment, with a family room, where we could get together at times.*" This was an impossible plan. Will knew that he could not build a large house on his salary. I would need to go back to teaching, and he had not gotten my approval. Also, his parents could not leisurely enjoy their own apartment within the house. We could not afford to employ a maid, a babysitter, and a gardener out of my teacher's salary. Will's actual plan was that I would teach, Clyde would become the gardener, and Laura would become the housekeeper and babysitter. Clyde and Laura were unaware of Will's real intentions.

Both Will and his mother were strong-willed, stubborn people, accustomed to getting their way. In the next year, Clyde and Laura sold their home, furniture, and many of their personal belongings. They packed only the items they would move to their new apartment in America. Then they took all of the economic and governmental steps needed for their visas and future security.

Will searched for a building site, escorted me to meet with prospective builders, and encouraged me to participate in the design of and materials for the house. He also found a future temporary babysitter for Dora. I was on my own to find a teaching job in August. I was hoping that it was too late to find work, but unfortunately, I obtained a position as an English teacher in a high school in San Jose, just in time for the opening of the school year in September.

The first day of school was heart-breaking for both Dora and me. The babysitter lived in the direction of Will's work, and my school was the opposite way. I remember Dora screaming as Will had to force her from my arms. She was still reaching out to me as he walked through the doorway. I was devastated. I had missed three months of her babyhood when I was in the hospital. Dora and I had had only seven months together since the end of my chemotherapy.

I realized that Will had made life-altering choices. He had chosen his mother to replace me to raise our child. He had chosen her needs over mine or those of our daughter. I felt like the "dishrag" my own mother had warned me not to become. Will was as happy as a lark with the plan that had been hatched. For him, the world was spinning merrily along as the sun and the moon sailed through space:

The Sun and the Moon

The sun and moon in the sky
Must have learned in the past how to fly;
> *They go sailing through space at a*
> *phenomenal pace,*
Tho' it seems very slow to the eye.

* * *

Returning to teaching was stressful for me, but I gradually adjusted to it, and Dora adjusted to daytime care at the babysitter's house. When our house was ready in May, we moved our pieces of furniture into a few rooms of our large, new house. The remainder of the house would need yet to be furnished.

At least I had the summer months to look forward to before Clyde and Laura arrived in September. There was time to enjoy Dora now and also time for marital intimacy. However, I was having trouble with responding, perhaps because of the anxiety of the past year or perhaps because of the uncertainty of the future. At the age of twenty-seven I had already gone through a sudden change of life. I remember the day after my hysterectomy. My breasts had suddenly hardened into painful stones. When the doctor came in for his daily visit, he explained that the sudden loss of the ovaries had produced a hormonal change, against which my body was rebelling. He dealt with it by shots of hormones and then prescribed estrogen suppositories. Still, my vagina had remained unhealthy and slow to respond to sex.

Will was unhappy about this, but he seemed to have forgotten my suffering and near-death experience just the prior year. We had no assurance that I would remain free of cancer until the next four years passed; meanwhile, he had committed us to the new responsibility with his parents. (After his death, I understood better that he had seen himself, not me, as the brave victim during this stressful time.) In an autobiographical record he had written:

The transfusions were continuing, but Beth suddenly started to scream in pain. I saw her hospital physician going by and called him to attend to my wife. He summed up the situation immediately, went to the nurses' station and finding no one there (!) mustered me into service. Grabbing a load of towels, he told me to keep handing him the towels as he soaked up the blood resulting from his pressing repeatedly on her abdomen. Pretty soon the doorway to her room was crowded with nurses. The doctor rounded on them that they had vacated the nurses' station and told them to "Get the hell out – her husband is doing a fine job." The immediacy of the situation is what kept me going, but finally, when he was finished, I had to sit down to avoid fainting.

* * *

Will's parents were scheduled to arrive in mid-September, and I was beginning to feel nervous about their living with us. I had not gotten to know them well when they visited the U.S., and Will expected me to turn over the care of Dora to his mother. It was already late August when Will relayed the history of his parents' lives:

Clyde was born in a little village not far from Peterborough. His father had been a farm laborer; his mother died when Clyde was three. Since his father never remarried, Clyde was raised by his sister, Maisie, who was twenty years older and cared for him like a mother.

Clyde received only a primary school education. However, he was bright and managed to educate himself through extensive reading. Some of his favorite books were classics by Charles Dickens. He liked math and taught himself arithmetic and beyond.

When he returned from serving in the army during World War I, he was hired by the brick-making company in Peterborough as one of their bookkeepers. Because he was dependable and diligent, he remained their employee until he retired.

In 1931, Will's parents married. Laura was not Clyde's first choice. His sweetheart was killed on the day of their wedding. As she was walking to the church in her wedding gown, she was struck by a team of horses pulling a heavy load of grain. Clyde never completely got over it. Years later, he met Laura when they both had roles in a local musical. Laura had a lovely, warm contralto voice, and Clyde was a lyrical tenor. Laura had had musical training, and Clyde had a beautiful natural voice, which he had learned to train by singing in the church choir. It was their love of singing and their talent that brought them together.

After they were married, they continued performing in musical theater. Laura liked the recognition they received from singing and acting, and when Will entered school, she began to take him to perform at various communal events. Will had a beautiful bell-like natural voice, but the frequent early performances ruined his tone, and as an adult, he no longer had a solo voice.

When Will paused narrating, Beth commented, "How sad for your dad to have lost his sweetheart on their wedding day, but if he hadn't, you wouldn't be here." Will nodded. "Your mother must have always wondered how she measured up to Clyde's first love."

"She never mentioned it. Her main goal in life was to be as perfect as she could in many ways. As a mother, she always strove for a clean house so that I could grow up in a healthy environment. That's one reason why I didn't get to know my Aunt Maisie well. She never married and became almost blind as she aged. Her house was too untidy and dirty for Mum, and Dad usually had to visit his 'mother' alone."

"That's sad. Will, what was your mother's family like?"

Will began by describing the lives of his grandparents:

Laura's father, William, was a prominent detective in the Peterborough police force. Laura was always proud of him; however, she was both proud and ashamed of her mother's background. Her mother, Annie, had been raised in a cottage on a 2,000-acre farm, where the squire (landowner) lived in the manor house. The squire was the civil magistrate for not only the farm laborers, but also for the residents in the adjoining village and the church that was located on his property.

When Laura's mother was a young virgin, the squire exercised his 'Droit du seigneur' (called the right of the first night: to deflower a virgin on his land on her wedding night.) If the maiden's sweetheart wanted to prevent the squire's right, he had to make a money payment to the squire. William was only a poor patrolman at that time and could not afford to pay the squire; so, Annie was deflowered and became pregnant. William immediately married her and took her away from the farm; nine months later, Laura was born.

Beth commented: "I didn't realize that England was still such a feudal society at that time."

"In some rural areas it was," answered Will. "I think that Mum is happy to have been born with upper-class blood in her veins, but she is also ashamed of it and cannot publicly acknowledge it. I think that growing up with the family story of the squire influenced her to constantly better herself and me. Because she was the oldest of eight girls, she had the leadership role. Following her general education, she attended business school and then found a job as a book-keeper and part-time manager of a floral shop. In addition to studying music, she took French lessons because the upper classes are bilingual.

"When I was a youth, she encouraged me to learn to play the violin and to study French. She wanted me to grow up to be a gentleman who was capable of going anywhere and conversing with anybody. The one thing she was ambivalent about was a university education. There was no academic college or university in Peterborough. Although she wanted me to have an advanced education, she wanted me to remain under her care because of my poor health. It was my father who helped me to further my education."

When Will finished his narrative, I felt like I knew his parents better, but I felt uneasy about Laura. She appeared to be a very determined woman. I wondered if our personalities would clash.

Chapter V: The Impossible Plan

School started for me towards the end of August. Dora was again watched over by the babysitter. As a family, we followed the routine we had established during the former schoolyear. We worked hard all week and then treated ourselves to a dinner at a restaurant on Fridays before our busy weekend schedule. We often went to Stickney's, a medium-priced restaurant, which served parents with children. Although Dora was 19 months old, she was usually well-behaved. I fed her first, and when she became sleepy, she curled up on my lap while Will and I had drinks, food, and coffee. Because he was a captive audience, this was a good time for me to converse with him. As his parents' arrival became closer, I became more anxious.

I began the conversation: "Will, you relayed the history of your parents when we last talked about them, but you didn't say much about their personalities. What are their characteristics?"

"My dad is a very good, steady, quiet, and reflective man. I never saw him be unkind to anyone."

"What is he like with your mother?"

"He is protective of her. Perhaps that stems from his tragically losing his sweetheart. Whenever my mum is in an angry mood, he doesn't defend himself or fight back. He waits quietly until she is calmer. Sometimes he goes out to the garden to work; sometimes he takes a ride on his bicycle."

"It sounds like he lets your mother take the leadership role in your family."

"Yes, by nature Mum is determined to make important decisions. When I was nine, she persuaded my dad to send me to the expensive Deacon's School for Boys, following my primary education. Attending and later graduating from there was a badge of honor. People from Peterborough could always tell who went to Deacon's because each boy wore a striped jacket with the Deaconian Crest on it. The crest symbolized the school motto: Whatever you do, do it well."

"It sounds like you were encouraged to do your best, Will, and to be proud of being able to go there."

"Yes, my mum was strict with me when it came to my studies and behavior, but there were times when she just let me be me and work things out for myself. I remember during the war, when I first started at Deacon's, my stomach and intestines reacted to a bad lunch. I messed my underpants, and I had to figure out how to handle the embarrassment. I went to the bathroom and washed them out in the toilet; I put my trousers back on and left the underpants in the corner. After school, on the playground, I found a fallen tree branch to use as a pole. I managed to attach the soiled underwear to the end of the pole, and I began walking home with the pole and pants slung over my shoulder, as if I were carrying a lunch and was on my way to fish in the River Nene. My mum came along on her bicycle. She had just come from the butcher to buy some horsemeat (the only meat available to us during the war). When she saw me, she stopped and said, "What are you carrying? You look like a regular hobo." I explained what had happened and that I was bringing the soiled pants home to be washed. (Clothes were rationed during the war.) Mum said, 'In a situation like that, Will, you should have just discarded them.' That evening at the supper table, she regaled my dad with the story, and we all had a good laugh."

"A cute story! It shows that your mother was understanding and could enjoy humor."

"Well, there wasn't much humor in our lives in the spring of 1943. I became very sick with a combination of illnesses: rheumatic fever, encephalitis, and pneumonia. When I became comatose, I was given a lumbar puncture and was not expected to live. After I miraculously pulled through, I was so weak that I had to stay in bed for six months. My parents hired a full-time nurse for me, and they took turns watching over me when the nurse was off duty."

"It sounds like your mother became very protective and needed to protect you," I said.

"Yes, as I slowly but gradually got better, Dad allowed me more freedom, but Mum tried to keep control."

* * *

When Clyde and Laura arrived in mid-September of 1964, Will and I turned over to them the care of Dora, the house, and the garden. Clyde became deeply unhappy within a few days. Unlike quiet, peaceful England with its few automobiles, he could neither bicycle nor walk into town, to church, to the "greengrocer" or to the park. Although he had enjoyed gardening on his own small plot of land, he was chagrined by our one-acre plot landscaped with plants with which he was unfamiliar and disliked.

Clyde became depressed, but Laura became a tyrant. In England, among her relatives, she had been nicknamed "Lady Laura." Before we were married, Will had proudly called her that, too. She had raised her son to be like her. She and Clyde had paid for his university education, and he had succeeded in becoming the first college graduate in his family. Unfortunately, she had not expected him to move to Canada. He should have married an upper-class girl and become a successful mathematician in England. Laura had laid a guilt trip on him about leaving home after all she had done for him. Furthermore, he had married an American who had come from humble farming ancestors. Now Laura was expected to become my housekeeper, maid, and babysitter. How humiliating it must have been for her!

Will was foolish not to realize that he was putting both his mother and his wife in an impossible situation. (Later, I learned from Clyde's memoirs that Laura had had a history of psychological problems: *She had a spell in the Chelsea Hospital for Women. Several times in the Middlesex, once in Guys, and was inmate at Papworth.*) If Will had told me about his mother's psychotic history, I never would have agreed to Will and Laura's plan. Since I was teaching during the day, I could not have protected two-year-old Dora from an unstable or explosive situation.

It was not long before the explosion took place. Will and I came home one Friday afternoon to find Laura in a rage. She had taken a message from the adoption agency which we had consulted before the plan by Will and Laura had been hatched. Directing her words at me, she yelled, "So you expect me to take care of someone else's God-damned brat in addition to yours!" I said nothing as Will gathered Dora and told me to take her for a ride.

When I returned with Dora hours later, Will relayed to me the dramatic story of what had happened: Laura attacked him on the stairs, trying to push him into a fall. He had wrestled with her and finally subdued her. She went to her bedroom, locked the door, and took an overdose of her sleeping tablets. Authorities had been called, had handcuffed her and taken her to a hospital for the weekend. Clyde had stood by throughout, wringing his hands and mumbling.

Laura was released from the hospital on Sunday evening with an appointment for a family meeting with a psychiatrist. It did not take the doctor long to analyze the situation. Laura directed most of her venom at me and accused me of subjecting her to a filthy disease. She had found my underwear in the laundry basket and had seen a discharge from the estrogen suppositories that I was taking at the time. I had no need to explain this to the doctor, who knew my medical history. His advice to Laura and Clyde was to go back to England, which were happy words for Clyde, but useless for Laura.

When we returned home, Laura informed us that she had no intention of returning to England. Will and I decided to seek the advice of my parents. After our call to them, they agreed to fly from Nebraska to help Will to convince Laura of her need to return. Until my parents arrived, Clyde and Laura kept to their bedroom. Later, after a lengthy conversation Dad had with Laura at our home, we were convinced that she had come to her senses.

My parents stayed a few days and helped them to pack. We all drove to the airport together. Mom and Dad's flight left first. As soon as their plane was out of sight, Laura turned to Clyde and said, "Good! Now we don't have to go back." Clyde was terrified and stood like a statue. Will immediately threatened to commit her again. She realized that she had lost the battle and joined Clyde on their flight to England.

Will never apologized for his mother's behavior or for their impossible plan. It had been an extremely stressful time for Will and me, and even worse for his parents. In Clyde's memoirs, he described this time as "harrowing." Their return home was embarrassing for both of them. Clyde relayed how they needed to explain the situation to people "over and over again" until he got "thoroughly fed up with it." Clyde never blamed me for the tragedy, but to Laura, I remained the "ugly American."

Although Clyde disliked the American culture, Laura disliked much more about the Americans: She resented the USA for succeeding the British Empire as a major power in the world. She thought it unfair that the U.S. had entered World War I so late, allowing England to shoulder the burden of the war. When World War II began, the U.S. had again waited until England was on the verge of destruction before the "Yanks" had joined the battle. After the war, England was left destitute while the U.S. had become wealthier and had chosen to help the country of Germany to rebuild rather than to help their ally, Britain.

Laura preferred the English system of education, which was geared to a distinction between those capable of only a general education and those intelligent enough to be admitted to the private system of the upper classes. The Americans were too egalitarian, trying to educate everyone.

America lacked the majesty and beauty of the former empire, which still existed in its palaces, stately homes, cathedrals, royalty, pomp and circumstance, the Houses of Parliament and other great institutions of law and education, formal English gardens, and an ancient code of chivalry.

She resented wealthy Americans who came to England to experience all of these things while demanding their three-minute boiled eggs, their cold beer, iced water, and fresh salads. They wanted a private bath adjoining their hotel room. They wanted the restaurants and pubs to be open whenever they felt like eating or drinking. They valued money and what money could purchase, like English antiques, instead of culture. But the Americans refused to learn the English system of coinage, with its pounds, shillings, and pennies, not easily converted to the decimal system of the U.S.

She disliked what the Americans had done to the English language. They had substituted words like "while" for "whilst" and "two weeks" for "fortnight." Will had agreed with his mother, that the English language was superior to the American. (Throughout life, he made long lists of American replacements of English words and refused to use the American replacements. He preferred "dustbin" to "garbage can" and "pub" to "bar"). Laura hated not only the American vocabulary, she hated the lazy, unclipped accent of the Americans, as they slurred the word "water" into "wad-der" instead of "wah-tuh."

Will remained in some ways an English "snob" in regard to language, and there were times when he purposely emphasized his English accent. Most of the anglophiles I knew admired Will's accent and his English ways, and he loved becoming the center of attention.

* * *

A poem he wrote reveals the superiority he felt for the English language:

English is the tongue which
Calmly, and without too much
Fervor, allows expression
Of the deepest thoughts of man.

The romantic power of the
Romance vernaculars is undenied;
Also, the precise and staccato
Majesty of the Teuton tongue is evident.
But there is a splendor in English:
There is the capacity for great beauty.

English, skillfully used,
Is a language of simplicity,
Of easy, pithy renderings
Of the mind's images,
Of the soul's yearnings and desires.
English is the language of poetry.

Chapter VI: Will, Beth, and Dora

From October of 1964 until November of 1967, Will, Dora, and I led a happy family life. Will was working at his fourth job since coming to California. With his education and his innate talents, this was probably the best job he had had to date. Litton-Mellonics, a sub-contractor through Aerospace Corporation, was supplying the U.S. government with Satellite Command and Control programs. Will's job was to use his mathematical skills to study existing code for computers (which at that time were slow and had little memory) and find number conversions to reduce time-costly looping. He became a hero at Mellonics when he wrote his "Bin, Fill & Spill" program, which reduced the loading time for the code by sixty-seven percent, making it possible for the U.S. to install a new antenna for a satellite.

I, too, now healthier and more energetic, was enjoying my work as an English teacher. My life was unbelievably busy. Three of my female friends from the English Department, their husbands, and Will and I met on Saturday evenings for a dinner at one of our houses. When it was my turn to be hostess, my week followed a typical pattern: school during the weekdays, grading papers Monday through Thursday evenings, dinner out with Will and Dora on Friday evenings, up early on Saturdays to clean house and prepare dinner for eight. Will helped me to entertain our guests and then clean up after the party. On Sundays we attended church in the morning. Afternoons were nap time for Dora and a time for marital intimacy for Will and me. After her nap, Dora always climbed into bed with us so that we could play "Patty-Cake" with her fingers and "The Five Little Piggies" with her toes.

On the weeknights when I was busy with schoolwork, Will escorted Dora to bed. Each night he stayed with her at her bedside and sang songs to her, such as "The Owl and the Pussycat," helped her with her prayers, and tucked her in. This routine led to a close relationship between them, one that has remained.

His darling poem, titled "Mr. Bear," is about the English teddy-bear sent to Dora by Clyde and Laura. Dora both loved and mistreated "Mr. Bear" throughout her childhood.

This is the tale of Mr. Bear,
Whose sad, sad fate was less than fair.

OBSERVER: *"Mr. Bear, Mr. Bear,*
What on earth are you doing down there?"

MR. BEAR: *"It's a sad, sad tale I have to tell –*
How out of bed I tumbled and fell.
I didn't really fall at all:
I was rudely thrown, as I recall;
My little mistress got hold of my arm,
(She didn't know she was doing me harm),
And swung me around and threw me out,
(I hit the ground with quite a clout),
I'm lying down here wondering when
I'll have the good fortune to be lifted again
To a position from which I can look around
- Instead of lying face down on the ground;
But I know the sad fate that's bound to be -
To be thrown around almost constantly."

During this period of Dora's youth, Will on special occasions became the "poetical Santa Claus" or the "poetical Tooth-Fairy." In preparation for Christmas Eve, Will and I joined together to find hiding places where Santa could leave his gifts. Then Will wrote a poem for each one, giving Dora clues for finding it. The following is from Christmas Eve, 1965:

> This year, sweet Dora, Santa brings
> Four pretty packaged play-time things.
> The first, though not so scary,
> Is really rather hairy.
> You'll find it in a sink,
> I think.
>
> The second is the Shepherd's cry!
> "Early morning, sky so red,"
> "Oh My!"
> You'll find it in a drawer,
> What's more!
>
> The third is awfully like the last;
> But now the sky is blue (not overcast).
> You'll find it under bed of sleepy head.
> (Don't wake him).
>
> The fourth is made of finest cloth
> (The kind to guard against the moth).
> This one is in a kitchen closet;
>
> That wasn't hard at all –

Or was it?
There are times you're not as good
As you should be;
But those times are rather rare
And Santa's fair.
He knows many girls much worse
Who strut and kick and curse.
So be better still my pretty lass
And please remember not to "Sass."
Grow straight and slim and kind and true,
Then there's nothing in the world
Too good for you.

*　　*　　*

By age six, Dora had figured out the game, and she had begun to write to Santa or to the Tooth-Fairy. When she had lost her sixth tooth, she left the tooth and a childish note for the fairy under her pillow. Fortunately, the Tooth-Fairy found it when she was asleep and responded by taking the tooth and replacing her note with his poem:

To the dear, dear girl who writes
such nice notes to the Tooth-Fairy –

The last little girl who wrote so well to me
was called Mary
- or was it Carrie?
Before your tooth I had collected five
trillion teeth.
Thanks so much for the sixth-
the special one –
now I have five trillion-six.

47

The last tooth was from a young
fellow called Heath –
-or was it Keith?
I'm so very forgetful –
I sometimes forget to show up –
Especially when my little friends
start to grow up.

Go show off, here's a buck
and lots of luck -
go have yourself lots of fun.

*   *   *

By Dora's birthday in 1967, Will's former "skiing lifestyle" had caught up with him. His aortic valve had calcified to the point where there was little room for the blood to pass through. Open heart surgery was still rare and not easily performed by surgeons, but Will had no choice if he wanted to extend his life. Surgery was scheduled for December, whenever a human valve (a homograft) became available.

We were both extremely worried. I was facing the likelihood of becoming a widow at age thirty-two with a six-year-old child to raise. Will was facing death and the day-to-day difficulty of keeping his job as his energy decreased.

Our marital intimacy suddenly ceased. Will plopped into bed one night, too tired to say goodnight. He turned over with his back to me and immediately fell asleep. I lay there, feeling anxiety for him and sorrow for us. (Unfortunately, after the surgery, when he had again regained his health, the lack of goodnight tenderness often remained.)

Waiting for this difficult and still experimental surgery to be scheduled was difficult. Since an aortic homograft would be used, Will was on standby until the hospital called him that a young, healthy person had become a victim of an accident and that they had permission to remove the valve. In preparation for the surgery, Will had to recruit his co-workers to donate a total of twenty pints of O-negative blood for the surgery. They gladly did this, making him again the center of attention at the office. None of them had known anyone who had gone through the bravery of having his heart stopped, operated on, and restarted again. One of the artists in the group drew a caricature of Will, and each of his co-workers signed it and sent it home with him on his last day before surgery.

The day of the surgery I sat in the waiting room from early morning until mid-afternoon. To keep my mind from worry, I marked up a stack of compositions. Because the surgery lasted so long, fluid had built up in Will's lungs. He had to overcome pneumonia as well as the reknitting of bone and tissue as he recuperated. After a long stay in the hospital, he was allowed to complete his healing at home. For the next month, he experienced difficulty breathing at night. After a tiring day of work, I frequently needed to bundle up Dora and carry her to the car for a 2:00 or 3:00 a.m. trip to the hospital to get help for Will.

* * *

By the summer of 1968, I was the one who needed to recuperate. However, it was a delightful summer I had with Dora – watching her learn to swim, playing with her in the sand at the beach, enjoying her playing "teacher" with

49

the children in our cul-de-sac. The children were all similar in age, but I was the teacher on the block, and that made Dora the likely one to play that role.

When school began again in the fall, we were all ready for it and for work. Now a second grader, Dora returned to the country private school we had chosen for her. In addition to academics, it was a place for her to experience the joy of riding horses and playing soccer. With private lessons on Saturdays or after school, we introduced her to music, first lessons in ballet, then piano, and later oboe.

In the summer of 1970, Will and I took Dora for a vacation to England, to re-introduce her to her grandparents and to see the country of Will's birth. Enough time had passed since their disastrous stay with us. I, too, was looking forward to seeing Peterborough and learning about its history and culture. Will's stylized poem, "The Nene" had given me a flavor of this area:

> The Nene a jolie river is;
> filled are her waters full of fish,
> that many an angler's lyne and rod
> hath landed strate upon the sod.
>
> Medeshamstede* lieth on her bank,
> which once beneath the Wash was sank;
> a port it was of fayre renowne,
> and latterly a busy towne;
>
> a camp nearby the Romans made,
> a ford across the river laid
> at Castor where the Nene is shallow,

and the pastures lush and fallow.

*the ancient name for Peterborough

*   *   *

Laura, who was the president of the local Bible Society, invited me to be the "Opener of the Summer Fayre" at the Town Hall. That meant my giving a speech. I chose the topic of English cathedrals, and I described my impressions of the cathedrals we had seen at Lincoln, Ely, York, and Peterborough.

Following the program, I was interviewed by a female reporter from the local newspaper. Midway in my discussion with her of an American's impressions of the cathedrals, the thatched cottages, and the beautiful green countryside I had bicycled through, Will rushed up, interrupted our conversation and turned the attention to himself. He droned on and on about all of the antique purchases we had made to furnish our large house in America, including a Victorian velvet settee with matching his and her chairs, a brass fender for the fireplace, and a silver tea service. He relayed our plans to have them shipped around the tip of South America to a port in San Francisco.

Silently I stood by, realizing the impending consequences of his pride. Although I was not a celebrity, an article in the newspaper the following morning included a picture of me and the headline, "American Antique Huntress in Peterborough." The vicious article described me as a wealthy American who had come to England to buy antiques, which would be shipped out of the country to America.

A family gathering and dinner were held at the house of one of Will's relatives in the afternoon. Everybody had seen the article. No one mentioned it, but I was ostracized. I took a corner seat and stayed there while Will happily mingled with his aunts, uncles, cousins, and their spouses and children. Laura had witnessed the event of the reporter's interview and neither explained it to the group nor apologized to me. Will did not admit that he had misbehaved either to his relatives or to me, who had become the "ugly American." Dora was too young to understand what had happened.

Following the day of the family party, Will and I were scheduled to resume our trip. We had planned to take Clyde and Laura with us as we traveled throughout Scotland. However, I was so hurt and angry with Laura's and Will's treatment of me, that I refused to go ahead with the trip if Clyde and Laura were to accompany us. Will did not argue with me about it. He simply told his parents that our plans had changed, and we traveled throughout Scotland alone. After we returned to Peterborough, we spent a final day with Clyde and Laura and then flew home. The numerous antiques we had purchased would be shipped across the Atlantic, through the Panama Canal, to San Francisco. From there, they would be sent by truck to our home in Saratoga.

* * *

The purchase of the English antiques began a period of materialism for Will and me. Our big house gradually began to look more like a museum than a home. In addition to the English antiques, we purchased American antiques, as well as Oriental carpets, oil paintings and watercolors, and pieces of antique chinaware. Church on Sundays was sometimes skipped for a weekend visit to galleries in San Francisco or Carmel. Gradually, pride replaced happiness.

We were headed in the wrong direction – not the direction of love for each other or love for God. Materialism left no room for gratitude: thankfulness for a life that had not been cut short; for science and the doctors who had been successful; for life in America, where open-heart surgery had been possible at this time; for friends and co-workers who had given of themselves; for a wife who had prayed for and stood by her husband during dark days and nights. It was as though Will had reverted to the self-gratification days of skiing in Colorado, and I was along for the ride. Will expressed this ride well in his poem about materialism:

Devil Drive

He was in limbo,
Wrestling with the demon spirits from Hades
  Who had it in their power to start their
  terrrible tortures
At the first sign of human weakness.

Before his eyes, and into his mind
Flowed images designed to tempt him:
Beautiful-bodied vamps beckoned him,
Cavorting in a lascivious cabaret;
Girls like these he had lusted after on earth,
But here in limbo, he was without interest.
  Sensuous, undulating forms now failed to
  move him;
  Failed to stir the consuming passions he had
  known before.

He looked, not with complete indifference,
But yet he was acquiring the immortal's
Imperviousness to carnal things;

> *Even when the demons produced*
> *magnificent spreads of exotic food, he was*
> *not to be swayed.*

He seemed aware that an immortal has
No need for even the necessities of the flesh.

The arch-demon had a new idea!
He and his hordes set to
To fabricate a wondrous thing:
A transcendentalised racing automobile!
When they had finished their creation
They beckoned their prey anew,
With smirks of satanic savvy on their faces,

> *Yes! He had to get in!*
> *He had to get behind the wheel and   drive*
> *this machine!*

Once in, he closed the door,
Positioned the seat, adjusted the mirrors,
Turned on the ignition, and pressed the gas-pedal.
As the machine accelerated, he realized
He could not control it. He could not escape;

> *He found himself hurtling through the*
> *gaping jaws of Hell,*

Found himself met by the hosts of darkness,
Lustily chanting their refrain:

> *Tried for lust;*
> *Lust and pride;*

Pride and lust;
Trussed and tied.

The devils congratulated Satan
That he had so cunningly contrived
And won the very soul of this and future Americans;
And Satan, in his own demonic heart,
Acknowledged the world's automobile designers
For giving the victim his preconditioned response.
He made a mental note to include them
In his latest "Who's Who in Hell!"

*   *   *

Chapter VII: Changes

Not long after we returned from our trip to England, Will moved from Mellonics to Fairchild Systems in Palo Alto, to a position where he would be a programmer and manager of a small group of systems analysts. When he turned thirty-nine in October, Will began to show signs of dissatisfaction with our marriage. Much of his discussion with me at home about his new job seemed to be centered on a co-worker named Victoria, whom he consistently described as "brilliant."

The company held its annual dinner-dance in the early spring – an elegant affair requiring the women to wear evening gowns and the men to be formally attired. For the occasion, I had purchased a lovely gown at I. Magnin in San Francisco. It was a white silk gown with a matching silk shawl. A purple flower and green-leaf Oriental-looking design spread along the bottom of the skirt. The white silk was embroidered with geometric elongated circles made of golden threads. It was fitted to the waist and then flowed freely from the waist down. The dress was perfect for my slim figure.

When I had dressed for the evening of the dinner-dance and presented myself to Will, I expected to receive a "Wow!" Instead, his response was, "Very nice."

At the ballroom, the party was divided into circular tables of eight. Will and I sat with the men he managed at work and their wives or girlfriends. Will dominated the conversation, leaving me to be one of the listeners. Much of the conversation was about one of the vice-presidents, Elton E., who had just left the company after undergoing several sex-change operations. A good-looking man in his forties, he had opened a transvestite bar in San Francisco. He had left his wife and three children and a successful job for a complete life-style change. He and Will had exchanged poetry while Elton was still with Fairchild; Elton's poems were filled with sexual eroticism and fantasy.

Although couples at our table were dancing, Will did not ask me to dance. However, when I returned from a trip to the "ladies" room, Will was dancing with Victoria. I watched as he escorted her back to her table and then took a seat next to her to continue their conversation. Returning to our table, he said, "Let's go." That was it – the end of an evening of sitting like a mannequin in a beautiful dress.

* * *

In the spring of 1971, a bad car accident began a series of changes in our family. Will, Dora, and I had met for dinner one evening at a restaurant. Afterwards, Will turned right in his car onto a busy street, and Dora and I turned left in my car. A truck driven by a drunkard came barreling through the red light and hit my car broadside, with the point of impact directly on my door. Will witnessed the accident in his rearview mirror and came running. Dora had been playing on the floor in the rear of the car and was thrown onto the back seat. She suffered only minor injuries.

When I saw the truck coming at a high speed, I knew that this was the end for me, and perhaps for Dora as well. At the impact, my heavy old Oldsmobile refused to overturn; it spun around and around, each time my head hitting the metal side of the door. By the time I was released from the car, my head was swollen to twice its size. Later, x-rays at the hospital showed no broken bones, but I was kept there until most of the fluid inside my skull had been released. (One orange-sized lump above my left eye took four months to be absorbed.)

The remainder of the spring and throughout the summer, I recuperated at home. A period of anxiety and depression set in. For three months, I had weekly sessions with a psychiatrist, first for the anxiety and then to discuss my experiences and feelings that had led to my unhappiness at age thirty-six. Dr. S. advised joint sessions with Will, who refused. Eventually, he agreed to meet with Dr. S. privately rather than as a couple.

On our way home from Will's meeting, which had followed my session, he reported that Dr. S. had found no need for another session with him – Will was well-adjusted! It was obvious to me that Will had not been forthright about his background or about our present life. At ages thirty-six and thirty-nine, we could still have developed a beautiful, loving relationship.

* * *

When I returned to school in the fall, I had been assigned two new classes and a room at the back of the gymnasium, which had no windows, but plenty of noise from bouncing basketballs throughout the day. By the end of the semester, I could no longer endure the glare of harsh electric lights, the noise, and the feeling that I was working primarily to maintain a large, richly decorated house. I resigned from public school teaching at the beginning of the new semester.

Will was not prepared for me to be just a homemaker. Perhaps he was worried about being the sole wage earner, and he didn't like the prospect of strictly budgeting; or perhaps he was comparing me with Laura, who had worked outside the home her entire life. Although I needed a rest, I was not allowed to have one.

*   *   *

Will soon found me a teaching position in the computer industry. I had just a month to take classes to learn the PDP-8 and then develop lesson plans to teach a week-long class for adult students, whose companies had purchased the new, small PDP-8. The course included training in the classroom and in the computer lab. It was a daunting task for an ex-English teacher. Will was working nearby in another company, but he came only twice to have lunch with me, preferring to play bridge with co-workers at lunchtime. On the whole, I was left to "sink or swim" on my own. Although my students wrote good critiques of my teaching skills at the end of their week-long training sessions, my manager felt that I was not advancing quickly enough. By the end of six months, he fired me.

Meanwhile, Will had become discontented with Fairchild and had decided, together with a group of programmers, to found their own company. They would each put in capital equivalent to the position that they would have in the company. Will wanted to be the chief scientist, and he convinced me that he would have enough capital if we re-mortgaged our house in Saratoga. With my income now gone, I encouraged him to wait for another opportunity to become an entrepreneur.

However, Will was a risk-taker. He had shown this in the past when he left his secure job in Canada for the dangerous ski slopes of Colorado. His poem, "*Nil Carborundum*," a rhyming acrostic sonnet, shows him to have been a seeker of dreams, oblivious of the cost:

N	*"Nil Carborundum"* was the merry cry:*
I	*"In very truth" – the damsel gave reply-*
L	*"Lift not your hands to tasks too strong for them:*
C	*Clean hands and hearts are the purest emblem,*
A	*And no virtue lies in flogging horses –*
R	*(Rivers should not wander from their courses,*
B	*But rather they should be quite regular)."*
O	*Oft-times I've heard these cries from way afar,*
R	*Resounding through my head and through my soul:*
U	*"Unless you watch out you will miss your goal –*
N	*Never will you have the chance to return –*
D	*Do what you will with haste before you burn:"*
U	*Useless to squirm and hope to dodge the cost,*
M	*Meaningless the fight when your soul is lost.*

* nil = Latin word meaning "nothing"
carborundum = a compound of carbon and silicon used in polishing

* * *

I, "the damsel," could not convince Will of the virtue of playing it safe for the sake of our family. He took out a large mortgage on our house (In eight years it had doubled in value), and we engaged in the struggle for the new company to succeed. Within less than a year, the company failed for lack of funds.

Since Will had no scientific problems to solve at the company, he created intellectual puzzles at home, either a mathematical problem to solve or a homemade device which could be taken apart and reassembled. Our closets were filled with these, with which he played and enticed others to try to solve. One of these puzzles he called Hi-I-Qubes, for which he wrote a twenty-one-page manual, with three pages of illustrations and eighteen pages of explanation. It was designed for players of only MENSA I.Q. (Will had taken the Admission Test for the American MENSA organization and had scored at or above the 98th percentile needed to become a member.) He did not join this exclusive club, but the test had probably given him ideas for his puzzle. Will hired a patent attorney, who tried to obtain a patent for Hi-I-Qubes, but the puzzle remained an unfulfilled dream.

Will could not remain out of work for long. We now had a bigger mortgage and no income. After a short time on the market, our large house in Saratoga sold at twice its original cost, and we moved to a much smaller house in Los Gatos, one which was in need of repairs and improvement.

Since we were both temporarily unemployed, we worked together to make improvements to the house. We laid brick on top of the concrete patio at the back of the house and slate on the walkway and porch in front. We tiled the entryway, the kitchen and bath counters, and the fireplace ledges. After Will had started a new job as an applications programmer at Atallah/Tandem, I continued remodeling our home by refinishing the woodwork and repainting the walls. Then I landscaped the front and rear gardens, leaving the beautiful tall Canary Island pines and deciduous trees, and planting camellia and azalea bushes and flowers in the gardens. When all of the labor was done, we felt proud that we had accomplished so much with so little monetary expenditure.

Before our move, we had worried about Dora's adjustment to a new house and a new location. We decided to keep her in the expensive private school during her sixth grade to allow her time for adjustment. The next year she changed to a public junior high school, where she needed to find a few friends among her classmates. We encouraged her to join the band, where she took up the oboe and found friends with an interest in music.

During Dora's junior high years, Will allowed me to enjoy my time as a homemaker and gardener. However, by the time that Dora entered senior high school, I wanted to reengage in intellectual pursuits. I began to take courses in law at the local junior college. With my skills in English, I thought of becoming a legal assistant. Since I had the time, I also took classes in math so that I could be more knowledgeable in Will's main subject field. This was rather short-sighted of me. He was so mathematically advanced, that when I asked for his help on a homework assignment, he was impatient and annoyed.

The legal knowledge I gained was helpful in later life. However, when Dora was beginning her sophomore year in high school, I used the math courses to my advantage. Louise, a teacher friend of mine, had informed me that the private school which Dora had attended was looking for a math and algebra teacher for their seventh and eighth graders. The school year was about to begin, and the principal was anxious to fill the position.

Headmaster Rutherford and I had a brief interview. From my resume he saw that I had a B.Sc. in Education from the University of Nebraska, an M.Ed. from the University of Arizona, fifteen years of teaching experience, and a California life-time secondary credential. Although English and music had been my subject fields, I was termed qualified to teach any subject in grades seven through twelve. Having recently reviewed high school math and done well in junior college math classes, I felt confident in accepting a teaching role in math and algebra for grades seven and eight. During the interview, Mr. Rutherford had primarily talked about himself instead of asking me questions about myself.

I accepted the position, but I knew that I would be answering to an intellectual snob in a "country school." He had come from a wealthy family, had attended an Eastern "prep" school before an Ivy League college, and had given himself the title of "Headmaster" of the school. In spite of his pretentious attitude, I enjoyed my work and did well, getting good year-end reviews.

During the second semester of my third year, I needed a substitute for a week because I was having surgery. Mr. R. came to our home for materials and plans which I had left with Will. That was the beginning of the end of my teaching career.

Will invited Mr. R. in and immediately began talking about himself: his degree in Pure Math from the University of London, his tutoring me in math in junior college, and his helping me with the algebra class I was now teaching. (Only once or twice had I needed help.)

When I returned to school, I sensed the Headmaster's coolness, but I didn't know then why his attitude had changed. Two weeks before the end of the school year, I had not had an annual review. I understood why when Headmaster R. came to my classroom at the end of the day on a Friday and told me that he was terminating me after the final day of the year – giving me two weeks' notice. He explained that I was not the kind of teacher he wanted on his staff.

Feeling that this was the end of my teaching career, I angrily responded, "If I am such a poor teacher, I wouldn't want you to put up with me for the next two weeks. I'm leaving now, not in two weeks."

"You can't do that!" he shouted. "Final grades are due!"

"Here's my grade book. You figure them out." I collected my things and walked out of the door. During the next two weeks, I had calls from board members and parents wanting an explanation. If Will answered the phone, he explained everything from his point of view. When I questioned Will about his conversation with Rutherford prior to my surgery, I learned that Will had bragged about his own expertise in math and had relayed that he had helped me when I needed it. Rutherford had decided that I didn't know math well enough to continue.

Chapter VIII: Searching for Happiness

During the last two years, while still teaching, I had accepted a part-time position as organist at a nearby Episcopal church. Having played piano since age five, I was a skilled pianist, and I had an innate talent for music. When Mr. J. left his position as organist, the rector encouraged me to work into the position. He was willing to let me temporarily use just the manuals of the organ until I could become adept at the pedal board. I knew enough about the difference between a piano and an organ to realize that learning to play the organ well would be a time-consuming task. But when I suddenly left teaching, I had all week to practice for a Sunday service.

When I began taking organ lessons, I found that playing the organ required coordination of hands, arms, feet and legs; building up new muscles; changing posture; learning different fingering and finger-substitution techniques; applying a smooth, legato touch instead of a percussive one; and reading music in a unique way. Unlike piano music, which is read with the mind assigning the treble clef to the right hand and the bass clef to the left, organ music is more complicated. For example, to read hymns for the organ, the mind must separate the music into three divisions, with the right hand playing the treble staff, the left hand playing the tenor part of the bass staff, and the feet playing the bass part on the pedal board. Solo organ music and scores for accompaniment are often written with three or more staves, requiring a simultaneous vertical/horizontal reading of the music. At age forty-one, I was learning to rethink thirty-six years of piano music while developing new physical skills for playing organ music.

I spent many hours practicing at church to learn these skills and to prepare for Sunday services, weddings and funerals, and anthem accompaniment for choir or vocal solos. Gradually, a male member of the church staff, seeing me daily, developed an interest in me. I was flattered at first but then became concerned that my marriage would be compromised when his advances became bolder. When I relayed this to Will and asked him to speak with my "admirer" or with the rector, he ignored my request. I wondered if Will was even a bit jealous.

One summer evening I found out. Will had invited Tom, a co-worker, and his wife for dinner at our home. It was a very hot night. We had had too many after-dinner cocktails. Tom suggested that we all enjoy the swimming pool. Will, unable to swim, and Tom's wife sat at the edge of the pool while Tom, in his boxer shorts, and I, in my bra and panties stepped into the pool. The night was dark, no lights were on, and Tom and I were enjoying the cool water. We had a playful but harmless hour of fun in the pool. After the couple had left, I expected Will to discuss the incident with me, but he did not mention it. He showed no jealousy or concern during that evening or afterwards.

* * *

Dora, now in her senior year at high school, had fallen in love with a boy named Vince, who had invited Dora to the prom. In preparation for the event, Will and I took them out for hamburgers and a discussion. We all enjoyed the conversation; they were looking forward to the prom, and we were enjoying their anticipation of the event. After lunch, Vince and Dora drove off in Vince's car, and Will and I headed for home in ours. I talked about Vince's handsome appearance and his wit; Will about Dora's beauty. I suddenly said to him, "As the mother of a beauty, at what percentile would you put me for women?" Without hesitation, he answered, "Fiftieth percentile."

I had never been a vain female. My mother had made sure of that, but I had always considered myself above average in appearance. I knew that his quick response had not been made in jest. Instead, it confirmed the actions he displayed when he flirted with other women in my presence.

Dora had begun developing into a beauty when she was almost fourteen. Will had secretly had a two-and-a–half by four-foot portrait painted of her. He had asked my friend Louise to allow a painter to come to her home for Dora's two sittings and to keep it a secret from me. Will planned to present the portrait to me at a surprise fortieth birthday party.

The evening of my birthday, Will took me for a ride. When we returned home, the portrait had been prominently displayed on a mahogany easel, placed behind the lower section of the Victorian settee. I pretended to be pleased. I did not really think it was a good idea to have a young girl as the center of attention in her home. Dora had already had enough adulation from Will. From childhood, he had often called her "Darling" or Sweetie."

*   *   *

During the summer of 1977, prior to Dora's junior year in high school, Will and I sent her to England to spend her two-month vacation with Clyde and Dora. I had mixed feelings about her flying alone. I worried about her safety and about how she would be treated in England, but I felt that it was a good opportunity for her to learn about Will's background and upbringing. I knew that the long separation would be emotionally difficult for me, but I also felt empathy for Clyde and Laura, who had missed out on learning to know Dora.

Clyde and Laura were overjoyed with her visit. They treated her royally in their home, and they gave her many opportunities to experience Peterborough and the environment. They also introduced her to a young woman and two teenage boys who were second cousins to Will. Dora was allowed to spend as much time with them as she did with her grandparents.

At the end of the summer, when Dora stepped off the plane, she looked like she had grown an inch and was several pounds heavier from all of the cake that she had eaten at teatime. She greeted us with an English accent, which lasted only a week before the California brogue took over.

* * *

In the fall of 1978, Will took a trip alone to be with his father, who had broken his femur. Clyde temporarily needed Will's help because Laura was in the Middlesex Hospital for psychological treatment. Since Clyde had difficulty getting around, they mainly stayed in the house. Will did the grocery shopping, fixed bachelor-type suppers, and helped Clyde to get adjusted to his crutches. When Will's two -week trip came to an end, he did not immediately return home, but took a trip to Wiesbaden, Germany. There he stayed in the apartment of a young bachelor, named Kurt, about whom Will had never spoken. When Will returned home, he had numerous photos of Wiesbaden and stories of the fun that Kurt and he had had attending folk music festivals, wine tasting, and a boat excursion down the Rhine. This was the first vacation that Will had taken without me, but not the last.

As a software consultant, Will frequently made trips within the U.S. to locations where he was sent by his company: El Paso, San Antonio, New Orleans, Boston, New York City, among them. He always came back with stories of good times he had had: a restaurant he had been to, landmarks he had seen, side trips he had taken; architecture he had enjoyed. He often extended his business trips to become a vacation.

When he returned home, he was emotionally exuberant but physically tired. By 9:00 p.m. he was ready for bed, and by 9:15 he was asleep. As a result, one of our problems was that he was often in a deep snore by the time that "my head hit the pillow," and I had difficulty falling asleep. When I complained about it, he moved from the master bedroom to occupy the guest bedroom at night. Later, when Dora left for college in the fall of 1979, Will moved permanently from the master bedroom. He was not unhappy about this solution. He could retire when he wanted, read in bed as long as he could stay awake, and turn off the light when he felt relaxed.

*   *   *

In 1980, Will's parents visited us in Los Gatos. Dora had spent a month with them in England in the summer of 1977, but I had not seen them since 1970, when I had been ostracized by the family. In spite of that incident, I was determined to be a hospitable American. While they were with us, Will and I hosted a fiftieth wedding anniversary party for them at our home. I did most of the planning, decoration, and work for the party. Clyde later described it in his memoir:

They gave us a right royal time. A reception was held around the swimming pool, and we were able to meet all their friends. Beth went out and bought card tables and chairs just for the occasion......

During their stay with us, they did not see the true relationship between Will and me. We turned over our master bedroom and bath to them to comfortably and privately enjoy. Will and I took the bedroom with twin single beds, and Dora, who was home from college, reoccupied her bedroom. When Clyde and Laura left to fly home to England, Dora returned to college, and Will and I again occupied separate bedrooms at night.

I made one more attempt at marital happiness by sessions with a woman psychologist, to whom I complained that Will and I were growing further apart, now that Dora was no longer at home. She encouraged me to convince Will to have joint sessions, but he emphatically refused. He felt that I was the problem in our relationship. When he had wanted to enter into an open marriage, I had refused. I thought that would end in disaster for our marriage. This was a turning point in our relationship. Unable to find happiness in love, I turned my hobby in music into a full-time career as a church organist.

* * *

When I was trying out stops at an organ studio in San Francisco in the summer of 1979, a former student of Richard Purvis heard me play and suggested that I contact Mr. Purvis to see if he would accept me as a student. A retired organist and choir master at Grace Cathedral, he was still composing choral and organ music, giving concerts, and teaching organ lessons. After auditioning me, he accepted me as a student. At about the same time, I began studying for a B.A and then an M.A in music at San Jose State University. Since the university did not have an organ professor on the staff, they allowed me to be trained in organ performance by Mr. Purvis, and I began traveling to and from San Francisco for organ lessons.

Mr. Purvis encouraged me to seek a better church position so that I would have an adequate instrument for practicing and performance. From a music major at the university, I learned of the opening for an assistant organist at a large Lutheran church near the campus. I was hired, and a year later when the organist left, I was hired to succeed him. The beautiful Schlicker pipe organ was a wonderful instrument for practice, for the worship services, and for the three concerts I was required to give for the degrees. In addition to directing the adult choir, I trained ringers for a bell choir. In the first concert that I gave to earn the B.A, I included several numbers for the bell choir. Will was not only a ringer in the bell choir, but also a singer in the adult choir. During my second concert, Will participated by singing a chant-like solo that I had composed for a composition class.

While I was busy with my music career, Will was a program manager at Ricoh, which had divisions in the U.S. and in Japan. Will had three Japanese programmers as trainees. From the first, there was a communication problem between them and Will. The three understood classroom English, but they had no idea of common American expressions. One day the three appeared in Will's office to ask him for the plans for the next phase of the program. Will, seated at his desk, arose and said, "I'm sorry. You've caught me with my pants down." As the three dropped their eyes to Will's ankles, he burst into laughter.

Will tried to improve their communication skills by inviting them to our home for dinner and taking them on sightseeing outings, which he asked me to join in order to enable more conversation. The young Japanese men were always very polite to me and thanked me for my hospitality.

In the fall of 1984, Will was sent by Ricoh for a six-week business trip to Tokyo. He extended the trip by two weeks so that he could take his annual vacation in Japan. When I watched Will board the plane for Tokyo, he looked quite healthy. Unfortunately, the young Japanese programmers were accustomed to following daytime work with evening pleasure. Will called me one night around 3:00 a.m. He was exuberant and so intoxicated that I could barely understand his speech. When I met him at the airport on his return, he looked haggard. He was not physically ready to face 1985, which turned out to be a very stressful and eventful year for us.

*   *   *

In February, on the Saturday of Lincoln's Holiday, twenty-three years after Dora had been conceived during our ski trip to Squaw Valley, she married Vince, her first love. It was a very large, expensive wedding and reception. The church was filled with local friends and parishioners and with relatives from the East and the Mid-west. I helped Dora with all of the plans for the event, prepared the pre-wedding and wedding music, and devoted myself to the guests before, during, and after the event. Will photographed Dora in many poses at home even though we had a professional photographer for the occasion. Dora wore my beautiful taffeta gown and a lace veil of her choice.

She looked gorgeous as she walked down the aisle with Will in a tuxedo.

The only sad point of the occasion for me was when the dancing began at the reception. Dora danced first with Vince and second with her dad. I sat watching and anticipating Will's dance with me, but we did not dance the entire evening

We had a recording of the ceremony taped so that Clyde and Laura could experience the event afterwards in absentia. In addition to the sermon and vows, the tape included the pre-wedding music by the bell choir, followed by my playing "The Voluntary In D" by Purcell as the wedding march and the famous Widor "Toccata from Symphony No. 1" as the recessional. Clyde especially enjoyed and appreciated the tape.

Fortunately, the tape arrived in Peterborough well before Laura's tragic fall. Clyde called us about it. Laura had awakened in the early morning and wanted a glass of orange juice. Although she was heavily dosed with sleeping tablets, she started down the steep stairs to get the juice from the kitchen. Clyde described it later in his memoir:

I was awakened by a loud bang at 5:00 A.M. on Thursday, the 12th of September. When I got to the stairs, the poor thing was at the foot of the stairs, with the side of her head smashed in. She tripped and tumbled down, smacking her head on a wooden hat stand at the bottom. She never regained consciousness.

The funeral for Laura was on the 20th of September. With the exception of Will, it was well attended by family and friends. Will did not fly home for his mother's funeral because he was afraid that the trip would be too strenuous for him. He needed a new aortic valve and a new pacemaker, and he was on standby until a homograft became available.

After a three-month waiting period, the surgery finally took place in late December. It was a very busy and stressful time for me. I had just finished giving my final organ concert for the M.A. and had accompanied a trumpeter from England for two concerts in the area. The day of Will's surgery was also the day of my final written exam at the university. Afterwards, I rushed to the hospital to see how Will was doing with his new homograft and pacemaker. I found him cheerfully sitting up in bed with an attractive nurse nearby. (Will was never too ill to charm the nurses.)

After a month of recuperation, Will was ready to return to work. However, instead of going back to the stress of Ricoh, he took a position as a scientific programmer in a pacemaker company.

Chapter IX: Crossroads

As a couple, we were at a crossroads. Will's mother had died; our daughter had married; Will had a new job and a new homograft. I had completed my degrees in music, graduating summa cum laude. I was still young enough to work towards a Ph.D. in Music, which I was considering. I looked into the programs at Berkeley, where I could have commuted and at the University of Arizona in Tucson, where I had gotten my M.Ed. degree. The latter would have required my living away from home. I had been paying for my own college expenses with the yearly income my father had been giving to each of his three daughters.

I was tempted to go to Tucson because I had enjoyed living there, and I would have enjoyed performing and researching in an area I knew. Also, getting a doctorate would have enabled me to acquire a teaching position at a four-year college and a prominent church position. I discussed these two possibilities with Will, who neither encouraged nor discouraged me.

I looked at the negative points of a separation: my parents would not understand my desire to continue my education instead of looking after my home; Dora would be left with more social responsibility for her father; the program would take me at least two years; it would be costly; and it would require a huge change in life for both Will and me.

When I analyzed my current situation, I found strong reasons to stay where I was. I liked my current church position. The parishioners were friendly and appreciative of my skills. The Schlicker pipe organ was a pleasure to play. But most of all, I loved our home in Los Gatos and was ready for a time to relax and enjoy it and the swimming pool and the garden.

It was fortunate for Will that I decided to end my student days. Will was laid off from the pacemaker company after only six weeks of employment. To compensate for his lower beginning salary there, he had been given generous stock options; the company now revoked this agreement, and Will lost his health insurance as well. He sought a settlement by hiring a lawyer. Meanwhile, we were in the dangerous position of being without adequate healthcare.

I took on a temporary position as a bank teller. The bank was close to the Lutheran church; so, I could retain my job there as well. My income from both paid daily expenses and the cost of healthcare insurance. Together with savings, we were able to make ends meet. Within a short time, Will received a handsome settlement. Not long after, he acquired a position to write software manuals for Honeywell Corporation. I was not expecting gratitude from him for what I had done. As the wife of an Englishman, I had learned that it had been my duty to keep a "stiff upper lip."

Since Will's new job would not begin until September, we had the month of August to travel to England to cheer up Clyde, who had been depressed since Laura's death. I resigned from the bank and obtained leave from the church to vacation in England. Flying into Heathrow, we rented a car, drove to Peterborough, and picked up Clyde for an eight-day tour of parts of England, including Boston, Norwich, and Bury St. Edmunds, and then across to Wales. Clyde and I became great companions. In his memoir, he wrote: *Beth so loved our country roads and villages. She sat with a map on her knee, and sometimes we got lost, but we eventually arrived at a town. Beth would find out the nearest cathedral or parish church, and, if possible, get a view of the organ. . . .Back in Peterborough, they gave me a birthday dinner at their hotel, which I shall remember always."* Clyde had just turned eighty-six.

By the end of the following May, he had died of prostate and bone cancer. In the last paragraph of his memoir, he wrote: *This house is much too big for me, but I shall carry on with it as long as I can. I have over one thousand color slides. I can turn any slide up at a moment's notice. I have a good library of cassettes, many of which are organ recitals by Beth. So, I have plenty of things to keep me interested.*

What a sweet man he had been! After Laura died, he tried to erase some of the bitterness she had left behind. In her will, she had left me a hand-painted fruit bowl, Dora quite a few memorable pieces of china and silver, but nothing for Will. Clyde had put Will back as the main recipient of his will, leaving him approximately fifty thousand pounds. Because Will knew how much I had grown to love his father, he bought me a beautiful antique diamond ring in remembrance of Clyde.

*   *   *

In June of 1987, we returned to England for Clyde's funeral. Dora came with us to honor her grandfather, whom she had learned to love during her time with them as a teenager. The funeral was well-attended. Clyde had been a tenor in the church choir for most of his adult life and had continued singing until his last six months. Following the service, Will, Dora, and I stood in a receiving line to greet parishioners who had come to the ceremony. No one knew me, but a few remembered Dora from her teenage vacation with her grandparents. One of the parishioners angered Will when he said, "Will, you didn't really know your parents well, did you." I silently agreed with the man. Will had not often communicated by letters or by phone, and his parents must have shared their sadness with their church friends. Secrecy and lack of communication do not create good relationships.

After the funeral, it took us a few days to go over what Clyde had left behind in his house. Dora selected a few items for keepsakes. Will went through the cassettes and photographs and packed up those that we would ship home. I selected a few of Clyde's Victorian novels to put into my suitcase. Will gave to his cousin, who was the executor of the estate, everything else to sell, give away, or keep for herself. She was also in charge of selling the house and following Clyde's instructions in his will regarding the assets.

Before we left England, we took a short trip with Dora to areas she had not seen as a teenager: first to nearby Cambridge, then to Oxford and Stratford-on-Avon, where we attended a performance of "Julius Caesar," one she was bound to teach in her high school English classes. She was bubbling with enthusiasm, Will was having a glorious time, and I was a "third wheel." When we were sightseeing, Will and Dora (having longer legs) kept pace with each other as we walked, and I trailed behind, even when crossing a busy intersection. At meals they conversed mainly with each other. Eventually, I had had enough. I said, "Tomorrow I'm leaving. I'm going home early."

"Don't be ridiculous!" was Will's response. We spent a very quiet evening together. Having discussed the incident sometime that night with her dad, Dora said to me the next morning, "I'm going back to Peterborough to visit with the relatives. You and Dad go on to London." Will and I spent time together in London, where we enjoyed a ballet, an opera, and a visit to Queue Gardens. Dora joined us for a final night out to dinner and a performance of "Les Miserables."

*   *   *

We returned to California in mid-July. I continued with my position at church, and Will adjusted to his new job at Honeywell. I was happy that it did not entail much traveling for him. He seemed to be happy working alongside American engineers.

*   *   *

In the spring of 1988, we had a European visitor. Kurt from Wiesbaden unexpectedly appeared on our doorstep. Now ten years older, he had remained a handsome, blonde-haired bachelor. Kurt was traveling in the U.S. and was only with us for a day and evening. He and Will obviously enjoyed each other's company, and I did not intrude upon their conversation. However, at the end of the visit, Will asked me to play a few Chopin waltzes for Kurt on the piano. Kurt politely listened to my performance. His only comment was to Will, reminding him of the folk music festival they had attended.

When Kurt left, I asked Will, who had liked only classical music, how he could have enjoyed the folk music festival when he was in Wiesbaden. A shrug of his shoulders was the only explanation I got for Will's 1978 mystery trip to Wiesbaden.

*   *   *

During the summer of 1988, problems arose at the Lutheran church, where I had been employed for eight years. A debate among the church leadership developed regarding the upholstering of the hard wooden pews. The older members of the congregation wanted the comfort of soft seats and backs. Those who appreciated music over comfort were worried about the effect of the upholstery on the acoustics.

I was asked to research the acoustical effect that the upholstery might have on the sound of the organ and the choral music. Will added his knowledge of physics to the report for the committee, which was composed of the clergy, selected members of the Board of Elders, and the financial officers of the church. The final meeting was held in an upstairs room. Will was invited to accompany me. After questions, answers, and debate, the committee voted to approve the upholstery.

Will hurled angry insults about lack of understanding and disregard for music, then stomped out of the room and stumbled noisily down the stairs. I sat shaken, the only female in the room, while the remaining males stared at me in amazement. When I had regained my composure, I left the room.

Throughout the summer, I was encouraged by members of various music groups, parishioners, and the pastor to remain in my position, but too much animosity had been created within the church. In the fall, I left for a similar position in another Lutheran church. Will joined the adult choir and the bell choir, which I again directed. However, I was careful to give him no opportunity to control my position, either openly or behind the scenes.

* * *

In September of 1992, our first grandchild, Sara, was born. Dora chose Will's middle name, Parker, as Sara's middle name, honoring Will and the English relations. I took two weeks off from church to care for Dora and the baby when they came home from the hospital in Manteca. My mother had helped me to recuperate from childbirth, and I wanted to carry on the tradition. I enabled Dora to get bedrest and to enjoy her newborn while I attended to their house and the preparation of the meals.

Vince was working parttime while attending college. He had dropped out of college when he and Dora were dating because he liked to party and did not take his studies seriously. Dora had graduated, had studied an extra year to get her teaching credential, and had taught for six years. Before they were engaged, Will and I had tried to get Dora to see that they were unequally matched and that she would have a big workload to carry if they married. But Vince was persuasive, and Dora ignored our warning. After they were married, Will and I helped them financially and tried to treat Vince well. However, he had not been able to warm to us as parents-in-law.

While I was in their home, I took over the cleaning of the house and the cooking. Vince made it clear to me that he had no intention of engaging with me at mealtime. Instead of sitting down to eat with Dora and me, he later prepared himself peanut butter sandwiches. For several days, Dora did not discuss his unwelcome attitude.

One morning, after Vince had left for work, Dora told me that Vince and she had talked and had agreed that she could handle Sara better on her own. She asked me to leave before Vince returned.

When I came home early, I poured out my hurt and grief to Will, but he had no empathy for me. In the months following, I did not try to make amends for something I had not done, and Dora did not contact me at all. I remained sick at heart. Will and I did not discuss the incident, but the estrangement must have bothered Dora because she reached out to me several months later to begin to repair our broken relationship.

* * *

In September of 1993, a year and a week after Sara's birth, my father died unexpectedly of a massive cerebral hemorrhage. By the time I arrived in Nebraska, he was still on a respirator even though he had been pronounced brain dead. Mother did not want to take the final move of having the respirator removed until her three daughters were with her.

I stayed with Mother for a month. Together we chose Dad's casket and planned the funeral and the reception following. Mother knew that because Dad had been such a well-known and respected businessman, many people would come to pay tribute to him.

Following the funeral, burial, and reception for guests, I stayed in Nebraska with Mother to help her with thank-you notes, business papers, clearing out files, etc. When I returned to California, I continued to call Mother several times a week to help her with her grief. I found that encouraging her to talk about memories of her years with Dad and memories of her own childhood and adult life helped her to temporarily feel better. As she relayed the past to me, I jotted down notes which I later used to write a family memoir.

My sister, Amy, who lived in Lincoln, convinced Mother to sell her property and move to a rental home near Amy. Mother made the move in December, but by June, she was deeply depressed. Loss of husband, home, church, and old friends were too much for her. I traveled to Nebraska again for a month's stay in Lincoln. By the end of the month, she had decided to move back to the area where she had lived for sixty-one years with her husband. There she would be among friends, living in a retirement complex.

During the two separate months of my absence from our California home, Will had had plenty of opportunities to be a "bachelor" again. He called me several times each week and seemed contented with his temporary "bachelor" status.

I was back at home by Christmas when my sister Nancy came for a visit. She was despondent from an unhappy divorce and was looking for a little joy and companionship. While she was with us, a bachelor friend of Will's appeared one evening for a visit. I had never met George, and Will had never mentioned him. Like Kurt, George was handsome and about ten years younger than Will. We decided to go to a dinner-dance restaurant for the evening. At a table for four, George sat with Nancy to one side and Will the other; I sat opposite George. The mealtime conversation was almost exclusively between Will and George. Occasionally, Nancy reached out to George, touching his arm at one point, but she received no response. No one danced during the evening.

When we got back home, Will invited George in; Nancy excused herself for the night; and Will then apologized to George for Nancy's behavior. *What apology was needed*, I wondered. I excused myself and left Will and George to themselves.

I went to bed thinking about our marital relationship. I thought about the evening we had just experienced and about the discussion that Nancy and I had had about our marriages. Her former husband had been openly unfaithful to her, but Will was secretive, and I did not know if he had been faithful to me. Nancy agreed with me that Will's refusal to see a marriage counselor with me did not inspire trust. We agreed that the reasons for Will's inability to share his feelings could probably be discovered by a professional.

Chapter X: Still Friends

From 1994 through 1997, our marriage continued on a friendship basis. Our common shared interests were church, music, family, and travel. During these years, we took delightful trips to Canada, including Montreal, Quebec, Banff, Lake Louise, Emerald Lake, Vancouver, and Victoria. One of my favorite spots was the Buchardt Gardens on Victoria Island.

Within the gardens, I was enthralled with a gorgeous tiered area that occupied a former quarry. It had been landscaped into different levels, with a path leading from the top level down to the bottom; thus, one could view the flowers and shrubbery from several aspects. If any place could re-ignite a romantic flame for me, that was it. However, I sat alone on various benches set along the path while Will took photos.

Will's favorite area was the large rose garden. Among the hundreds of varieties of roses were many individual plants named after famous people from England: members of the royalty, prime ministers, actors and actresses, musicians, etc. I was surprised at Will's interest in roses. For years, I had expressed my love of roses and had often wanted a bouquet of roses or even a single rose for my birthday. Will had always claimed to be allergic to them.

I had fond memories of visiting rose gardens with Clyde when we took him on an eight-day trip after Laura died. We often sought out a beautiful English garden within a town. With arms linked, we strolled along the paths bordered with flowers.

After Will's death, I pieced together the knowledge that roses had had a double meaning for Will – the flower and a lost love. In 1958, several years following his emigration to Canada, Will had returned to England for a summer vacation and had fallen in love with Gisela. Laura had encouraged the romance, thinking that Will, then twenty-five, would want to settle down in England. But Will wanted Gisela to leave her family and join him in Toronto, a move which she refused to make. Her rejection of him had put her on a pedestal. Unlike the American girls he was soon to pursue in the "skiing world," she remained pure.

His poem, "English Roses," had not been addressed to her, but the date coincides with that of a picture of Laura and Clyde standing next to Will and Gisela, with their arms around each other. A brief notation underneath the photo in the album read, "Vacation at Skegness" – one of Clyde and Laura's favorite seaside holiday spots.

"English Roses"

I gave my love on Monday
A rose of scarlet hue:
Elusive as the pimpernel
My wayward rosebud grew.

I gave my love on Tuesday
A perfect crimson rose:
To hint how much I loved her
- A fact which well she knows.

And then again on Wednesday,

A blood-red rose I gave –
Despair became my portion:
The love for which I crave.

I gave to her on Thursday
A rose of purest white –
A token of surrender;
My prayer throughout the night

That when I came on Friday
A carmine rose to give;
My prayer would have been answered
- Our nourished love would live.

And Saturday came smiling,
The rose a brilliant red:
My happy heart was laughing
- Our love by no means dead.

On Sunday I stepped gaily,
A golden rose my gift:
Its purpose in the giving
To end and heal our rift.

*   *   *

In the summer of 1998, Will and I had one of our most enjoyable vacations at Emerald Lake in Canada. It was not far from Lake Louise, a renowned vacation spot in the Canadian Rockies. Lake Louise was close enough to drive to if we wanted bustling activity. Most of our time was spent in the quiet and peace of the resort at Emerald Lake. Its name described the emerald color of the water, which was caused by the mineral content in the melting snow from the surrounding mountains. The water was ice cold.

Although we rowed on the lake, we were careful not to capsize. We also enjoyed hiking around the lake, which was not too large for an afternoon of exercise. After a hike, we enjoyed a drink by the fire in the lodge and then dinner in the restaurant. Fresh game was always on the menu: elk, deer, caribou, buffalo and also pheasant and quail and fish from the lake. My favorite entrée was caribou, and Will liked the more gamey taste of the elk.

Each bedroom was in a separate rustic cabin. Since there were no televisions or computers in the bedrooms or in the common rooms, Will could not climb into his shell of self-entertainment. Consequently, we read books, played cards and backgammon and engaged in **conversation.**

* * *

After we returned home from Victoria, Will began to experience symptoms of prostate enlargement, including frequent urination and high PSA levels. Following an examination and tests by a doctor of urology, Will was diagnosed with stage-one cancer of the prostate. It was a fast-growing cancer, and by the time that Will had surgery, the cancer had spread to surrounding tissue. Radiation treatment followed and then hormone injections.

One medical problem which definitely plagued Will following his surgery was urinary incontinence. When minor surgeries for this were unsuccessful, Will resorted to the use of the Cunningham Clamp, which can be manually attached at the base of the penis to prevent leakage of urine. Since leakage does not occur when the body is in a prone position, the device can be unclamped at bedtime.

Will endured some discomfort when using the device, but he enjoyed explaining the device to others, such as at a table of poker players one evening at Vince and Dora's. Will suddenly withdrew an unused Cunningham Clamp from the pocket of his sports coat, showed it around the table, and asked the men to guess what it was. When Will explained it, the look on their faces was a combination of shock and disbelief. They did not have the reaction of sympathy that Will had expected. Perhaps he should have also handed out a copy of his acrostic sonnet, which explained the device and his brave way of coping with it.

"The Cunningham Clamp"

C   *Can there be anything more beautiful –*
U   *Unless, with care, you look beneath the skin –*
N   *Noticing pregnant pods and fruit within –*
N   *Nothing less than pain's end: and so begin*
I   *In peace and love and spirit dutiful*
N   *Not to think bad thoughts, but each sad-glad day,*
G   *Gaining more acceptance, in ev'ry way*
H   *Holding on to truth for truth's sake:*
A   *And still the piper's costly fee to pay –*
M   *Making the best of unspeakable times.*

C   *Come! Snap out of morbid soliloquies! –*
L   *Leave behind "sad sack" groans for better climes*
A   *And smiles and laughs your downcast visage take,*
M   *Making yourself and others happy. 'Tis*
P   *Pantagruel's achievement – fresh water lake!*

*   *   *

In 2000, when Will had his third open heart operation, surgeons were no longer using homo-grafts from cadavers; consequently, Will's valve was replaced with a St. Jude titanium valve, which required him to be on a blood thinner for the rest of his life. Once again, I had to be nursemaid and mother as he awaited his surgery and then recuperated from it. It was more difficult for me this time at age sixty-five. I was finishing my career as a musician in a church where I had worked for ten years. At the same time, we were preparing for a move to Manteca, to be near Dora and her family. I had planned for the moving van and Will's operation to be at least two weeks apart. However, the hospital rescheduled his surgery for moving day, and I found myself trying to be at two different locations on the same day.

After Will was released from the hospital, I drove him to our new home in Manteca, where the moving boxes were waiting in the garage while our furniture was temporarily stored in a warehouse. Will was unable to help me as I unpacked each box and gradually turned the house into a home.

Since our grandchildren would be at our home a good portion of the time, we had purchased a sizeable house with a living room that was large enough for our grand piano. The first floor of the house also had a dining room, a kitchen with pantry, a bedroom with full bath, and a sitting room. On the second floor were a master bedroom with bath, two more bedrooms with bath, and a very large workroom with bookshelves, cabinets, and counters for desks. At the opposite side of the room, there was space for television, end tables, coffee table, and sofas or lounging chairs.

Outside there were a garden and patio in front and a swimming pool, half bath, patio, and garden in back. The house and the outside were designed for children to work and play.

Although our new house was lovely and modern, it did not have the charm of our home in Los Gatos, where we would have happily remained if Dora had not needed us to be nearer. We moved from quaint, delightful Los Gatos to the less cultural, rural town of Manteca to help both Dora and Vince with their hectic teaching and parental schedules.

Vince was now employed as a math teacher in Danville, fifty miles from Manteca; Dora was employed as an English teacher in Tracy, twenty miles from home, and their three children were attending different schools in or near Manteca – one in pre-school, one in lower elementary, and one in upper elementary. Will and I took on the roles of maid, babysitter, and chauffeur. Once he had recovered from his surgery, he resumed his job as a technical writer from his home computer; consequently, most of the care of the grandchildren became my responsibility.

My daily schedule was hectic: I had to be dressed for the day and have breakfast ready for Sara by 6:00 a.m. when Dora dropped her off on her way to the babysitter for Robbie and the preschool for Sue. Since school didn't begin for Sara until 9:00, I monitored her homework and piano lessons after breakfast and then prepared a bag lunch for the day. Once a week, I gave Sara a piano lesson. If time permitted, Will and I played cards with her, alternating between Knock-out Whist, which Will's father had taught him, or Old Maid or Seven-up, which my mother had taught me. At the end of the day, I picked her up from school, helped her with her homework at our house, and then allowed her to watch television or to read. Two years later, Sue was also with us in the mornings, and four years later, all three were with us.

My weekly schedule provided little free time for me, but I did not want to give up professional music, and so I accepted the position of Organist and Choir Director in a church in Turlock, about thirty miles away. While the kids were in school, I drove to Turlock to practice the organ or to prepare choral music. One evening per week, Will and I attended choir rehearsal at the church. Saturday was both organ practice and housekeeping day for me, and Sunday was church for both of us.

In my music position, I was asked to give an annual organ concert at the church. This encouraged me to keep up my technique and skills, and I usually followed the concert in Turlock by giving a similar concert at the Episcopal Cathedral in Reno, Nevada, which was an enjoyable weekend outing for Will and me. In addition to these public concerts, I helped the grandchildren to prepare a family recital at Thanksgiving or Christmas-time. I combined these occasions with a family dinner while Will prepared a cute program on the computer. All in all, our lives were extremely busy, but happy. Will and I felt needed, and we were enjoying the children.

Our contentment did not last. Robbie needed surgery when a tumor attached itself to his pituitary gland. By the time of his first surgery in San Diego, the tumor had grown to the size of an orange. Since the pituitary is located at the back of the skull, the surgeons had to split his skull from ear to ear, lift up the brain, and then remove the tumor. A year later at age six, the surgery was repeated because the tumor had regrown. When it regrew a third time, Vince took Robbie to Boston for three months of radiation. The hospital there had a machine which could pinpoint the radiation from the height of two stories, enabling more accuracy and less damage to the brain. Although the tumor did not regrow, Robbie lost his pituitary gland, which is the major control of all of the other glands and organs within the body. As a result, Robbie was left with a lifetime of daily replacement medication and expensive follow-up examinations.

All of this took a tremendous toll on the other members of the family. Dora and Vince became very protective parents, and Will and I sometimes felt as though we were "walking on eggshells." We tried from time to time to lighten the atmosphere for the girls by taking them on excursions away from home.

When Sara was seven and Sue three, we took them on outings close to Manteca, sometimes to play miniature golf in Modesto, sometimes to a nearby small zoo. When they were a year older, we ventured to San Francisco to see Fisherman's Wharf or to go for a boat ride on the bay. On one occasion we were on BART (Bay Area Rapid Transit), sitting close to the rear door of the car. When the train halted at one of the stops along the way, four-year-old Sue sprang up from her seat and was nearly out of the door before I could grab hold of her dress.

On another excursion, when Robbie was well enough to accompany us, I drove us to San Francisco for a day at the Exploratorium Museum for Children. Will's job had been to plot the location of the museum on a map from his computer and to navigate once we were in San Francisco. That day he was in one of his "wot not" moods. He couldn't find the location, and yet he wouldn't take suggestions from either Sara or me. We wandered around for several hours, with Sara and Sue calling out street names from the backseat. At one point, we had to stop at a convenience store so that Robbie could urinate. The store had no restroom! I had to shelter Robbie from view as he relieved himself against the wheel of the car. We finally gave up on Will's map, which was incorrect. (Will's map showed the Exploratorium located on a street that didn't exist.) Stopping at a gas station, we got the correct location of the museum, arriving in time for a visit of a few hours before we had to head home. The children had enjoyed the whole experience as a lark! Will's humorous poem, written in 1960 about famous Englishmen "wot-nots" still reminds me of Will and his map:

"James Watt and Christopher Wren"

James Watt
Knew not what.
He wot not.

Christopher Wren
Thought that Big Ben
Should be built again.

Thomas Carlyle
Thought it the style
To philosophize awhile.

The Elder Pitt
A man without wit
In Parliament did sit.

(Since Will's death, our grandchildren have often remembered him as a bit nonsensical. They enjoyed his "wot-not" characteristic and his high intelligence expressed in "quirky" ways.)

* * *

In 2005, Sara graduated from the eighth grade. She received the top academic award at her graduation ceremony. The principal, knowing how Will and I had participated in her achievement, thanked Will and me for our generational help. We were grateful for his acknowledgement. We did not often receive verbal thanks from Vince or Dora. However, on Father's Day and Will's birthday, Dora showed her gratitude by "going to town for him," (as Clyde would have said.) She invited us for dinner and prepared Will's favorite entrée, roast beef topped with Yorkshire pudding, and his favorite dessert, bread pudding. When a new local shop carrying English specialties opened up, she took him out for an afternoon English tea.

Towards the end of our time in Manteca, Robbie and I were invited to enjoy a tea occasion with Dora and Will. By the end of the tea, consisting of a pot of tea for each of us, tiny sandwiches, and trays of sweets, we were all stuffed. Will took the opportunity to recite one of his poems:

"On Overeating---"

The signal that the meal has ended-
The candles blown – the guests unbended,
Standing up and groaning so:

95

You've eaten far too much you know!
Your figure slim . . . before the feast,
But stay content – you're full at least;
Forget the line so smooth and pretty –
You can't eat more . . . and more's the pity.

Chapter XI: The Octogenarian

Each year when school was over for the summer months, Dora and Vince were again in fulltime charge of the children. Will and I were alone once more and took the opportunity for a summer holiday, each year going somewhere far from Manteca, such as Germany, Austria, or Switzerland. Now older, we both felt more comfortable on group trips where the planning was in the hands of the tour guide.

On our first evening in Frankfurt, we met Carl, a single retired Latin teacher from upper New York State and his cousin, Father John, a priest from Toronto. They invited Will, but not me, to spend the evening with them. I politely objected, and for the remainder of the trip, we often became a group of three men and me. I was capable of discussing their like interests of religion, art, music, literature, nature, geography, and history. There were a few bawdy jokes and stories with me in their presence, but I managed to keep our small group politely social.

We stayed friends for years, visiting each other in our individual homes in Manteca, Toronto, and the Finger Lakes area of northern New York State. Before Fr. John died a year later, we took a grand tour of Italy together. This time, Cora, Carl's female, single cousin joined us, having just retired as a teacher. We traveled throughout Italy on a bus. Since there was a daily rotation of seats, we asked the tour guide to arrange the chart so that each of the five of us could have equal visitation opportunities as we traveled. I noticed that Will engaged in lively conversation when he sat next to Fr. John, Carl, or Cora. When Will was next to me, he insisted on the window seat, turned away from me, and took pictures throughout the ride. When we stopped to tour a site on foot, Fr. John and Cora, the slowest walkers, stayed together while Will, Carl, and I walked ahead. It was not long before Will took off on his own with his camera.

Our trip ended in Venice. We five spent most of the last day visiting St. Mark's Cathedral. During an afternoon snack and a rest in the cathedral square, I asked Will to take me for a ride in one of the gondolas parked nearby. Being a romantic, I had visualized that experience for years. Will ignored me. I waited patiently for a break in the conversation and then repeated my request. Finally, after about five entreaties, Fr. John said, "Will, for heaven's sake, take your wife for a gondola ride!"

Since Will couldn't ignore_him, we headed for a gondola. The ride was a romantic disaster. Will immediately got out his camera and took photos throughout the ride. When we returned to the others, who looked questioningly at us, Will simply remarked, "The water was green and polluted."

After Fr. John died, Will and Carl remained friends until Will's death. They corresponded regularly through the internet. Both enjoyed serious religious and secular topics and, contrastingly, humorous, off-color articles. Will enjoyed sending Carl poems he had written, such as his "take-off" on "The Owl and the Pussycat," which was his nightly song to Dora when she was a youth.

"A Harlot and a Bishop"

A harlot and a bishop went out one day,
In a coach with a team of four,
They stopped in a field of fresh-mown hay –

And the bishop he opened the door.
She chased him around, and was gaining ground –
What a strange, strange sight to see:
And there in a wood, the harlot she stood –
And the bishop had climbed up a tree,
A tree --- a tree!
And the bishop had climbed up a tree.

*   *   *

In March of 2013, my mother died at the age of 100 in a nursing home in Nebraska. Although I had been expecting her death for some time, I was not prepared to have her finally gone from my life. To me, she had not only been a mother, but a friend, confidante, nurse, helper, teacher, and guide. She was the last of her generation within our family.

For the funeral, I flew to Nebraska with Dora. Following the funeral and the burial, I expected there to be a reading of Mother's will while my sisters and I were in Nebraska. However, the administrator of the estate avoided discussing the will or any financial matters.

A month later, when we had already returned to our separate homes, he informed us of the changes that had been made to Mother's will when she was already well into dementia. My parents had jointly planned for each daughter to receive one of their three farms, leaving the choice of the farm up to each of us.

Although the estate had been rich in liquid assets as well as property when Mother entered the nursing home, there was no longer enough cash to settle it when she died eighteen months later. Consequently, the administrator planned to sell one of the farms for the needed cash, making it impossible for each daughter to receive one of the promised farms.

Will was as unsettled with this scenario as I was. Since California is a community property state, the farm would become his as well as mine. When he married me, he knew that I would eventually prove to be a good economic "catch." Now we needed to work together to secure our economic future. We hired a Nebraska lawyer, who subpoenaed financial records which he then sent to us. Will and I became a team. I organized all of the material for the next six months, and Will mathematically analyzed the data and recorded it on the computer. Together we used his skills in math and analysis and mine in English and organization to produce some convincing documents and charts to be used in a lawsuit. Nine months later, we settled the estate without needing to go to trial. Will and I were now owners of a farm.

* * *

In 2014, with two grandchildren in college and Robbie about to finish high school, Will and I were no longer needed as substitute parents. It was time to move from our big house in Manteca to a humbler home. After researching different geographical areas within the U.S., we chose Santa Fe, New Mexico because of its beauty and culture. Not long after our move, we found a spiritually alive and musically satisfying church to join.

During 2015, we entertained family visitors to Santa Fe. In June, Dora came with Sue and Robbie for a five-day visit. All went well during the first three days. We took them sightseeing in Santa Fe, including the cathedral, the plaza, and Museum Hill. Then we introduced them to surrounding areas.

The second day we visited the Bandolier National Monument, where the ancient cliff dwellings are located. While Will sat on a bench, Dora, Sue, Robbie, and I climbed up wooden ladders to explore the inside of the dwellings. On the third day, after a beautiful drive through the Jemez Mountains and Los Alamos, we stopped for hamburgers in a restaurant on our way home. Dora kept searching for information about our decision to move from Manteca to Santa Fe. Will did not respond, but I finally said that we wanted to experience another geographical area since we were no longer needed in Manteca.

We all went to bed that evening with more plans for sightseeing the next day. Early the next morning, Will excitedly awakened me, announcing, "They're leaving!" I put on my housecoat and walked into the living room to find everyone dressed, ready to go. We sat down for a moment, and Dora explained that they were leaving because I had been unbelievably unkind to them. Turning to Will, she added, "Nobody ever likes Mom." Will turned white, but he said nothing. Dora, Sue, and Robbie had all of their luggage ready for a quick get-away. Without saying goodbye, they picked up their bags and left.

As Will began to sob, I admonished him for remaining silent and not supporting me. "Dora's words were cruel," I said, "and by your silence, you accepted them. Will, I am your wife! I have stood by you for 55 years. Remember our marriage vows: to love, honor, and cherish."

Will left the room and sat down at his computer in the workroom. A few hours later, the telephone rang. It was a call from Sue, who explained that they were on their way back to California. I was still in the living room, but I could hear Will's shout: "You'll be sorry for this!" That was not the kind of support that I had hoped for.

In the five months that followed, there was no communication between Dora and us. Will and I said little about the matter. However, the estrangement simmered in my mind, like a cup of coffee brewing on the stove. I thought about my lost time with Dora when she was a baby, and I was too ill to take care of her. After Clyde and Laura had returned to England, I had remained in teaching and had become too busy to give Dora as much attention as she needed, while Will had developed a bond with her, one that remained in Dora's memory as lovely bedtime singing and verses from Santa and the Tooth Fairy. After Dora had married, she wanted to be home with her children but couldn't afford to be, and I had replaced her, thinking that I was helping her by caring for the children.

I mulled over the ugliness that had taken place between us and came to the conclusion that she was blaming me for encouraging Will to move away from Manteca to Santa Fe. Although she and her family had had little time for us after the children were in high school, Dora wanted us to be near. Actually, the decision had been a joint one. Until now, Dora had not included Will in her silent treatment, and he was not accustomed to dealing with it. I decided that it was up to me to repair the rift. For Dora's birthday in November, I suggested to Will that we send Dora yellow roses as a peace offering. He was joyous, and we agreed that two dozen roses would look beautiful. When the bouquet arrived, Dora gladly accepted our gift of love.

* * *

Our second family visitors were my sister Amy and her husband Mike. Will and I again became sightseeing tour guides. I prepared a private organ concert for them at the church because they had never heard me perform. Since it was not a public concert, Will did not bother to listen to it but wandered about the church environs taking pictures and visiting with anyone in the area.

One evening the four of us sat down after supper for a game of bridge – a big mistake! Since his college days, Will had been an aggressive bridge player. In Toronto he had played duplicate bridge, had entered, and had won tournaments and awards. After we were married, he continued playing against the computer, read daily columns in the newspaper, and wrote poems or entered notes about bridge in one of his many notebooks on various topics.

I had been interested only in social bridge, played mainly for fun. Throughout the years, we had played bridge at times with my parents and sometimes with a church or social group. Years earlier on a visit to Nebraska, we had played with Amy and Mike, and because of Will's aggressive style and skill, we had "trounced" them. Will was looking forward to a similar event this time.

However, Amy and Mike had become duplicate bridge players. I had not played for years and could barely remember much about bidding. As the game progressed, Will became increasingly angry with me, insulting me and scowling at me. Letting the devil have his way, I suddenly bid <u>eight</u> No Trump, an impossible bid. Will threw down his cards and almost struck me; Amy and Mike laughed.

This scenario describes what to me was a petty incident, but to Will it was a blow to his ego. (Among the autobiographical sketches that he wrote before his death was one that he had titled "Will Takes Up Contract Bridge"):

Soon after I arrived in Toronto, I joined a bridge club that met twice a week at the west end of Bloor Street. To get there from Orchard View Boulevard I took the subway train down to the Bloor Street streetcar and took it to the Bloor Street west terminus. This took an hour each way.

Being a newcomer, I was paired with an individual who analyzed every play to the nth degree. I played with this person for about three months and grinned and bore it. Then the organizers of the club decided to have an individual tournament. My erstwhile partner came in second from bottom, but I came in third from top. Guess what! – One of the top five players adopted me as his regular partner. After that, we 'placed' at every meet, sometimes first, but never lower than third.

So, what is the golden rule for playing bridge? Have a solid understanding of the game, choose a good partner and trust one another.)

I was neither a good choice of partner for him in bridge nor in any other intellectual game, with the exception of Scrabble. After our guests had gone, Will left a sarcastic message on his computer in full sight for me to see: "Marriage is like a deck of cards. In the beginning all you need is two hearts and a diamond. By the end you wish you had a club and spade."

When I first read this, I stewed about it for a while. Then I realized that losing so badly to Amy and Mike had wounded Will's intellectual pride. Throughout most of his lifetime, he had striven to improve his skills in bridge, and I had made him look foolish.

*　　*　　　*

During Christmas of 2015, my niece Maggie and Sylvia, her nine-year-old daughter, flew from Nebraska to visit us. Maggie was especially interested in spending time in the cathedral and the square in downtown Santa Fe, and in hearing me play a short organ recital for her at our church. Maggie, a professional violinist, had brought her fine violin with her, and we enjoyed playing violin and piano together. Will, always addicted to his computer, never came into the living room to listen to us. Although he had once been a violinist, he had not played for years and was not interested in watching Maggie perform. However, he was interested in displaying his skills in poetry and in a series of creative "happy face" pictures he had made on the computer. Nine-year-old Sylvia found these amusing.

Maggie had appreciated the high-desert terrain of Santa Fe, ringed by mountains, and the wild plants that grew here. When she showed an interest in Will's poems about nature, Will wrote a poem in sonnet form * which he dedicated to her. It describes Will's favorite cactus on our rural lot:

"Cholla"
(a sonnet for Maggie)

Cholla is a cactus of great beauty
Here in New Mexico's desert landscape –
Growing sometimes to fifteen feet in height;
Yet a plant that whispers, "Do not touch me!"
Its spines can be a painful reminder –
"Touch me not!" it says again and again –
Sharp merciless spines imbed in your skin –
Not a sweet memory or loving touch!

Ecoutez-moi – I can't stress it too much!

Still its great beauty makes up for its pain –
Rosy blooms appear mid and late July
On its spiny stretched-out limbs and branches,
Whisp'ring, "Enjoy me – I'll soon disappear!"
Nascent harbingers of its yellow fruit.

* *A sonnet is a poem containing 14 lines with 10 syllables per line.*

*   *   *

After Maggie and Sylvia returned to Nebraska, Maggie called us weekly. If Will answered the phone, he always had five or six of his poems to read to her, some of them passionate poems from his Colorado skiing days. He did not reveal to her the name of the person to whom he had dedicated the poem, nor the year he had written it. Maggie naturally assumed that his passion had been for me.

"Hopeless Passion"

I fell in love with you –
So quickly – could it be true?
And yet to me it seems
That you're too often in my dreams.

I'm loath to understand;
Yet on the other hand
There's not a girl I've ever met,
Who on her own I'd rather get.

We talked for just an hour,

And I was in your power:
I loved you then as no one else could –
I loved you then as I never should.

After Will had read this poem to Maggie, she said to him, "You must have really loved Aunt Beth," to which he answered, "Oh, I wrote that for a friend of mine who needed some inspiration."

Chapter XII: Final Days

In May of 2016, I made one last attempt to divert Will's attention from the computer back to me. I needed to visit my farm in Nebraska, and I suggested to Will that we include the farm on an extensive car trip throughout the Midwest, driving to areas we had been many years prior or to some we had never seen. It was a long trip through Eastern Colorado, Kansas, Missouri, Wisconsin, Michigan, Iowa and Nebraska. From St. Louis, we followed the Mississippi River north to the Great Lakes area. While in St. Louis, we stayed at an elegant five-star hotel overlooking the Mississippi River. Our room on the tenth floor had a breathtaking view of the river barges and bridges at night. Our cat, Lovey, enjoyed looking out of the picture window at the activity below.

I had suggested taking 17-year-old Lovey along for companionship, hopefully to inspire some tender moments for Will. Lovey was like a tonic. While I drove, Lovey, sitting on Will's lap, encouraged him to love and to be loved. Will was quiet throughout the trip, but it had had a positive effect on our relationship. Sometime after our return to Santa Fe, he wrote a message for me on his computer, leaving it again in full sight for me to find:

"I thank God for my wonderful, accomplished, fun to be with, loving wife of 56 years, many of them difficult, but with her many capabilities we have overcome the vicissitudes, and I look forward to a healthier and happier life for us both in 2017 and beyond."

Not long after we were back from our trip, Will reverted to his dual personality, the public Will and the private, self-absorbed Will. In public he was an extrovert, seeking attention from even strangers when he recited one of his poems. At church he sought the attention of attractive women for conversation or praise for his reading of the Old Testament or the Epistle lesson of the day. At home he communicated via the internet. The house was often silent.

Will's false public display of regard for me was revealed one Sunday at the coffee hour following church. I was visiting with a friend of mine when Will interrupted our conversation by putting an arm around my shoulders and kissing me on the cheek. My friend exclaimed, "What a sweet, loving husband you have!" I had had decades of this kind of pretense, and I spouted out the truth: "He only does that in public!"

Once I had called him out on his behavior, it was not long before he ceased to be polite towards me. Already frail in health, he frequently needed me to drive him during the night to the emergency ward where I waited for him on a metal chair until he got the diagnosis and subsequent care he needed. He did not thank me after these long vigils. Sometimes he was admitted for an overnight stay in the hospital, and I was able to go home to my own bed. When I returned the next day for a visit, I found him cheerfully engaged with a nurse or a visitor, and I sat nearby as an onlooker.

A serious fall in the autumn of 2017 landed him in the hospital again. After a series of tests, the doctor determined that a blood vessel had broken in his right lung, which had filled with a pint of blood. When Will regained the function of his lung, they released him but had scheduled him for a series of further tests.

A week after his eighty-fifth birthday in October, we received news that Will had bone cancer, a metastasis of his earlier prostate cancer. We saw a doctor who specialized in radiology; the cancer, he said, was too advanced for treatment by radiation. Various oncologists were consulted, hormone treatment was tried, but the cancer continued to advance rapidly.

Will did not give up. He began to use the computer like a detective, looking for bits of information that would lead to a cure. Day after day, he sat quietly at his computer desk. Eventually, he had too much pain to sit for long periods of time.

One night at home, Will had an attack of anxiety. He angrily demanded that I immediately drive him to the hospital. This time they gave him oxygen and then assigned him to a room. I returned home. Following a two-day stay, he was released and taken by ambulance to The Beehive, a terminal care home in Bernalillo. I drove to the care home, signed papers, and watched as Will was hooked up to an oxygen machine and made comfortable in his room. When I bid him goodnight, he did not respond.

The following day was the 57th anniversary of our wedding. I attempted to create a spirit of celebration. Knowing how tasteless the food would be at the care home, I ordered two take-out meals from a fine restaurant in Santa Fe. Since the entrée was beef, I purchased a mellow bottle of red wine to accompany the meal. I loaded into my car a laundry basket with the food, wine, cloth placemats and napkins, along with chinaware, silverware and two crystal wine glasses. Right before I left Santa Fe to drive the seventy miles to Bernalillo, I stopped at a florist shop for flowers and a memorable vase.

When I arrived at The Beehive, Will was sitting up in bed and reading. "Happy 57th Anniversary!" I greeted him. He gave me a lukewarm smile. Since he did not want to chat, I opened the wine and offered a toast: "To the happy times in our marriage." We clinked glasses, but he did not respond with a toast or comment. I unpacked the laundry basket and set the bedside table with placemats, napkins, and silverware. I placed the roses on a table nearby. I opened the containers of food, loaded our plates, and handed one to Will. To me, the aroma of the beef was tantalizing, but Will did not appear to be at all hungry. He toyed with his food, but drank his glass of wine.

After dinner, we watched a movie on television, and I began to get ready to leave. Will had been quiet all day. I tried again to trigger a discussion of our 57 years of marriage by apologizing for any times that I might have upset him, but he refused to crawl out of his shell. I gave him a kiss on the cheek, picked up the basket, and left.

The next day, he needed to talk to me. He wanted me to buy him a laptop computer, have a member of the Geek Squad come to our home in Santa Fe, copy everything from his home computer onto the laptop, and set up a communication ability between the two computers. It was a tall order, but I thought that he was planning to email me when he needed to communicate with me at home. I purchased the laptop and accessories, had the copy and the set-up accomplished, and delivered everything to him within several days. He began fiddling with the laptop immediately, forgetting to thank me for the purchase, process, or effort I had taken.

I gave him a few days to adjust to it, and then I asked him if he had gotten used to his new device. He answered that it was too unlike his home computer, and he probably wouldn't use it. This was hard for me to believe of a man who had spent most of his adult life with various computers and was an expert at developing and using software. I suggested that I call a member of the Geek Squad to visit him in his room, but he said, "Just let it go." (After he died, I gave the laptop to our grandson, who found that Will had been communicating with the home computer. Will had deleted some files, changed some, and had e-mailed and sent copies to various people via the home or laptop computer.)

During the last five weeks of Will's life, a daily routine developed: Visitors from Santa Fe came in the morning. When Will was alone, he read, wrote, watched television (or used the computer). Medical visits and care from the staff were around the clock. I visited in the afternoon, bringing him his requests for special food or other items. While I was with him, he enjoyed playing Scrabble, a game requiring little verbal communication between us. I watched him eat his evening meal and then left to get home before dark.

Will's reading choices were probably unusual for someone close to death. I had purchased him a mystery for diverting his attention from self and also a spiritual book for comfort and meditation. He ignored these. He read his daily devotionals on biblical passages, but he devoted most of his reading time to a thick volume of 17th and 18th century English poems, which was given to him by a female anglophile from church.

He continued to write poems of his own on his laptop. As late as three weeks before his death, he retained the mental ability to write an acrostic sonnet about his cancer:

"Prostate Cancer"

P	*Prostate cancer is no laughing matter,*
R	*Reappearing out of the thinnest air.*
O	*One has surgery eighteen years earlier,*
S	*So it is a shock when it reappears –*
T	*To think it can lie dormant for so long*
A	*And is just lying around, ready to*
T	*Take possession of the skeletal bones,*
E	*Ending my life – a shout, not a whimper!*
C	*Cancer! – we are fighting you tooth and nail*
A	*Although it is true there are times like this,*
N	*Now for me, when the facts are dour to me,*
C	*Causing panic and unrelenting pain,*
E	*Each day praying for the ending to come,*
R	*Rejoicing that I'm still Your much-blessed child!*

His final poem, "The Sun," was written a day later. Some of his earliest poems, written in England, had religious subjects, as did his last verses. He had come full circle.

"The Sun"
an octet poem

The sun shines brightly in the sky –
Giving light to all the earth –
Making plants thrive and grow

113

Food for animals –
Also for man
To prosper
And thank
God.

*   *   *

During the last three weeks of Will's life, his visitors were neighbors who were friends to both Will and me, members of the clergy who administered spiritually to him, and Matt, a member of the men's book club. One day, close to the end of Will's life, Matt was just leaving as I entered the room. Will said excitedly to me, "Don't let Matt go. He's the only one who can keep me from the gates of Hell!" I did not have the opportunity to ask Matt what had led to that outburst.

Will remained extremely restless the remainder of the day. I stayed a little later than usual, just in case. To try to help him emotionally, I picked up the hymnal I had brought from home and began singing some hymns to comfort him: *The King of Love My Shepherd Is; Fairest Lord Jesus; Breathe on Me, Breath of God.* Will listened at first and then turned away from me. I asked, "Shall I continue? Does singing help?" His answer was, "No. Your voice is past it."

I said goodnight and left. The next day, when I told him that he had hurt my feelings, he had no response. However, he asked me three questions that day, which revealed to me that he was closer to death: The first, "Who is that person standing in the closet doorway?" There was no one I could see. The second, "Who are those people looking at us from the other side of the wall?" "Do you know them?" I asked. "No." The third, "Do you see the wall moving up to the ceiling light?" That was the last of our oral communication.

Before I left Bernalillo, I sought the advice of the manager regarding Will's hallucinations. She informed me that it was time to make a decision regarding the continuation of Will's medication and his life support. Will had signed a *Do Not Resuscitate* form. His kidneys were shutting down. The doctor advised an increase of morphine while Will's body naturally succumbed to death.

The next morning, having alerted friends not to visit, I arrived early. The manager met me in the lobby and told me that Will had had a very bad night. He had stood up in bed, had demanded to be taken to the hospital, and had needed to be medically subdued. He was better this morning, she said, and had apologized to her for his behavior, saying "I'm glad that I had the chance to get to know you."

When I entered his room, Will was lying silently and did not speak to me. Throughout the day, I ministered to him as he lay in fever. The oxygen machine, set at its highest output, could not supply what his body needed. I alternated between moistening his feverish lips with a swab and putting the nasal oxygen inserts directly on the lips of his open mouth. He did not look at me during the day or indicate that he wanted to communicate. He did, however, speak briefly with the clergy who visited in the late afternoon.

After the priest had left, Will began to jerk violently and sporadically. I held one of his hands securely and chanted over and over, "Lord have mercy; Christ have mercy; Lord have mercy."

Around 6:00 p.m., an attendant came into the room and said to me, "He's dying. Time to remove the nasal inserts." Will was staring with eyes wide open, looking terrified. As I removed the inserts, he violently jerked one final time. The attendant walked to the window and opened it, saying, "The soul sometimes escapes through the window." She left me alone with his body. I sat there with conflicting feelings. I was glad that the suffering for him was over, and the anxiety of his impending death for me, but I still wanted him to reach out to me, to explain why he had hidden so many of his feelings from me.

It was hours before I could leave. First the medical examiner had to come, then the mortician, the hospice care worker, the manager of the home, and finally a resident member of the clergy. When I finally got back to my home in Santa Fe, I called Dora in California to tell her that her father had died. Tearfully, she exclaimed, "Thank God. He's out of suffering." She paused. "I'm so glad that I got to say goodbye to him."

"When was that?" I asked.

"The priest who was with him called me. It must have been when you were out of the room. Dad couldn't speak, but he could hear my voice. The priest told me that Dad smiled faintly as he listened."

I was too exhausted to speak for very long with Dora, but our telephone conversation caused me to reflect about the last time that Will, Dora, and I had been together. Shortly after Will and I 'celebrated' our anniversary, Dora and Sue took the opportunity of their winter holiday from school to fly to New Mexio. I drove to Albuquerque to pick them up at the airport. From there we went directly to The Beehive. Will was ecstatic. He was temporarily eager for conversation, and then he suggested a game of Scrabble. Since Sue had never played the game, I became her partner and helped her to learn the tricks of the game. The score was close, but Sue and I won. When we left to drive to Santa Fe, Will had hugs for Sue and Dora. I stood by.

The next day we each took Will gifts – Dora and I gave him pajamas, and Sue presented him with a collection of family pictures of "Grandpa," which she had made into a booklet. Nothing could have pleased him more. Later that day, when we left for the airport, the final goodbyes were heart-breaking, both for them and for Will.

After driving Dora and Sue to the airport, I returned to Will's room instead of going directly home. I had decided to surprise him by an unexpected visit. This time he didn't ignore me. We talked about Dora and Sue for a while, and then I put on my coat to go home.

"Stay here tonight," Will said. "You can lie next to me on the bed." Perhaps he intended at last to share some of his feelings with me. Unfortunately, I responded with reasons for not staying: I had not left lights on at home; Lovey needed care – food, water, his sandbox changed; neither of us would sleep well; he needed to rest.

"Will you at least kiss me?" he asked. I walked to his bedside and gave him a light kiss on the lips; he did not reach out to touch me. I said, "When I was a child, I was taught to say a nighttime prayer which frightened me. I still include it in my nighttime prayers, but now it comforts me." I recited it:

> *Now I lay me down to sleep;*
> *I pray Thee, Lord, my soul to keep.*
> *If I should die before I wake,*
> *I pray Thee, Lord, my soul to take."*

117

I asked him, "Did you say that prayer as a child?" He smiled slightly and shook his head *no*. I waved goodbye and left. A tender time like this never returned.

Chapter XIII: Stages of Grief

A week before Will died on February 5, 2018, at the age of eighty-five, I had met with a representative of a funeral home/crematorium from Albuquerque. I paid for the final expenses to include a private family service at the home before the body was to be cremated. Dora and I had agreed that we would both like to see Will at rest. While Vince and Dora were on their way to Santa Fe, I made the arrangements for the viewing.

Since Will would be cremated in a casket, I chose a cloth-covered composition one of blue; the top would open only for the upper-third portion of the body while a large bouquet of various-colored flowers would cover the remainder of the top. I had chosen two green plants to be placed on pedestals on either side of the coffin. I agreed to take to the funeral parlor my choice of attire for Will: khaki pants, his favorite tan corduroy jacket, a dress shirt he had liked, and his Deacon's School tie.

On February 10th, when Dora, Vince, and I walked into the small private viewing room, Will looked peacefully asleep. He had been bathed and shaved, and his hair had been washed and combed. My last vision of him with mouth open and eyes staring in fright was now replaced with that of a man who is no longer in a struggle to live. Dora read a few excerpts from the *Bible;* Vince took pictures; I stood by the casket.

When the attendant came in, I asked him to explain what would take place in the coming days. The cremation would occur four days later, after the surgical removal of Will's pacemaker. Will would be cremated in the casket, along with his clothes and the bouquet of flowers. The date of the cremation would be February 14th, which ironically fell in 2018 on Valentine's Day and Ash Wednesday. (Two days later, Dora and Vince would celebrate their thirty-third wedding anniversary. It would also be the fifty-eighth anniversary of Dora's conception during the Squaw Valley skiing weekend for Will and me.)

When Dora and Vince flew home, I began to tie up the loose ends of my life. For the next three months, I was too busy to be mired down in grief. Louise, a friend for fifty-five years, had died in early December and had named me the trustee of her estate. I had helped her in 2000 at the time of the death of her close companion, followed six months later by the death of her only child. We had been frequent visitors to each other's houses throughout the years; in her later years, she had often stayed with Will and me for long periods in Manteca.

Her estate had been large, but her California lawyer was neither well-organized nor trustworthy. After repeated difficulty in communicating with him, I hired my own lawyer in Santa Fe to help me to deal with the estate. Paying bills, gathering information, dealing with forms for business and healthcare, refunds, selling stocks, paying taxes – all became part of my life. Meanwhile, I was also dealing with Will's papers, records, and finances as well.

During Will's final year of life, I had been the president of a women's group at the church. In addition to overseeing activities and planning for the 2017-2018 year, I prepared a series of lectures on "The Psalms" for our monthly meetings. I had begun working on these during the summer, researching historical sources, studying The Old Testament, taking notes, and arranging the materials into chapters. I planned to provide hand-outs from five to ten pages, as needed, for each of the lectures. When Will was still at home, he did not like my using <u>his</u> computer. He stood behind me or sat in a chair close by. If I asked him for computer help too often, he insisted on taking over. Will had selected a password for his computer, which he would not share with me. Later, at The Beehive, he finally gave it to me when he needed to have the transfer made from his home computer to his laptop.

During early May, I needed to plan the details for Will's memorial service, which would be held Saturday, June 2nd, at the church, with a noontime reception following in the parish hall. Although the hospitality committee would take care of all of the physical arrangements for the reception and provide the majority of the food and drinks, I decided to order special sandwiches from a local bistro, enough to provide for the reception and for a later gathering of family members at my home.

The bulletin for the service also needed my input. I confirmed Will's choices of the choral anthem, "God So Loved the World" by Stainer and my chant-like composition of "The Lord's Prayer," which Will had sung at the close of my second master's recital. I approved of his selection of hymns, including "The King of Love My Shepherd Is," the first hymn I had sung to Will the evening he was so agitated in the care home. The gospel lesson he had chosen was John 10: 11-16. (Jesus said) "I am the good shepherd . . . I have other sheep that are not of this fold . . ." Will's belief, of other sheep being saved, was the cornerstone of his mother Laura's religious views.

I had chosen a picture of Will to be placed at the end of the bulletin. Taken the day of Dora's wedding, Will was standing in front of a row of books in our Los Gatos home.

He looked eternally handsome in a grey tuxedo with a carnation in his buttonhole. The opposite page of the bulletin contained a biographical sketch I had written, ending with, "God bless Will today and always."

When I had finished the preparation for the service and had presented my final lecture on "The Psalms," on May 15th, I had just thirteen days before Dora and Sue would arrive for Will's memorial service. I suddenly had time for the emotions that I had kept bottled up. I realized how alone I was. The house seemed spooky to me and, I felt that Lovey, our cat, was acting eerily. (Later, I wrote about it in a poem):

"Ssssh!"

Sweet Lovey,
resting peacefully
on the sofa;
Suddenly leaping
to the floor,
yowling,
Standing, staring,
puzzled or
remembering?

Searching place to place:
the bathroom,
the computer desk,
the bedroom,
the shower.
Sadly, I watch him.

I can remember the form

he is searching for:
standing at the sink,
sitting at the computer,
sleeping in the bed,
showering in soothing water.

Sensing, like Lovey,
is beyond me,
belonging to a cat's world,
belonging to a
Spiritual world which is his, not mine.

*   *   *

I couldn't sleep for days. One night I was overwhelmed with panic and anxiety. I called an ambulance to take me to the hospital. I couldn't sleep there either. The second day, automatic muscle massagers were wrapped around my legs, sleep medication was given to me, and I slept. I was released to go home the next day.

The hospital had given me material to read about coping with grief. Before Dora and Sue arrived a few days later, I learned that when the death of a loved one has been anticipated, the one left behind can feel physically and emotionally exhausted. The frantic activity of the last three months had kept me from dwelling on my grief, but it had taken a toll on me.

When Dora and Sue arrived, they stayed in the house with me to give me company and to help me to prepare for the next events. While they were with me, Sue handled meals, calls, and e-mails. I gave Dora one of the articles on grief I had read, knowing that she was experiencing deep feelings of loss for her father.

Dora had brought with her twenty condolences that she had received from friends and relatives. One of the messages to her was from her daughter Sara: "He loved _you_ more than anything in this world. He was so proud of you. He adored you to pieces and you got all the best pieces of him." This one hurt me. I knew that it was true, but I had yet to learn how to live with the truth.

I felt that I needed to share with Dora a stack of sixty condolences sent to me, personal notes indicating that I had been well-liked, even loved by relatives and friends, along with Will. As Dora read through some of these, I hoped that she would see me in a new light.

Family members arrived in groups: the rest of Dora's family (Vince, Robbie, Sara, and her husband from California); my sister, Nancy, and her family (one daughter from Texas, a second daughter and grandson from California); Maggie came alone from Nebraska.

All went well the day of the memorial. The service was well-attended. It was a beautiful spiritual event – the music was glorious; the sermon, prepared by Father Andrew, captured the earthly Will and his immediate family, along with the encouragement to look ahead to the eternal. Then we all gathered in the memorial garden as Will's ashes were put into his niche in the columbarium.

Dora, Sue, and Maggie had helped me to set up a memorial table of pictures, albums, and items representing Will's life. The food tables had been arranged in the shape of a cross and had been decorated with flowers. I had hired a pianist to play light classical music and tunes from musicals during the reception, which provided the right atmosphere for relaxed conversation.

It was a beautiful June day for the family gathering at my home. The garden had been planted with colorful flowers along the front path and in various pots. Most of the family chose to enjoy their refreshments in the garden. The next morning my sister Nancy and her family left; later in the day, Dora and her family said goodbye. Maggie stayed with me an extra day to ease me into my world of being alone again.

After the family had left, I had more time to reflect on Will and our marriage. Will and I had been such different personality types. He was a mathematician, a fact-finder; I was a romantic. He lacked sensitivity; I was too sensitive. He constantly sought new information; I was goal-oriented. He had been allowed to become a self-centered child; I had learned to share with two sisters.

A confidante of mine suggested to me that writing about my thoughts and memories would help me to understand my emotions and feelings about Will. Since Will had expressed himself so often in his poetry, I decided to put together a collection of his poems.

Chapter XIV: A Bouquet of Verse

Will had put together a booklet of his earlier poems, and I gathered together the later ones which I found on the computer or around the house or on scraps of paper at The Beehive. All in all, I discovered around 100 of his poems, which I studied. I selected 65 of his "best" ones for the collection, which I entitled *A Bouquet of Verse.*

Will's poems were as varied as his personality traits had been. Some of his poems were rhymed, some unrhymed; some were pithy, some detailed; some of the forms were in standard paragraphs, some were designed creatively to give a pictorial effect on the page.

Throughout our marriage (1960 – 2018), the form he liked the most was the sonnet, probably because of its difficulty of poetic expression when using an exact number of lines (14) and an exact number of syllables per line (10). Out of the joy of making it even more complicated for himself, he sometimes chose to make a sonnet acrostic, so that the reader would have to read the poem both vertically and horizontally. Will wrote five of these, including his last one, "Prostrate Cancer."

Will also made a sonnet more difficult to write by making the lines rhyme. One of these, "The Programmer," he based on Rupert Brooke's famous poem, "The Soldier."

"The Programmer"

If I should die, think only this of me:
That there's some corner of a salesman's field
That is forever programmed. There shall be
Beneath false floors a richer dust concealed –

A dust who programs wrote, debugged and ran;
Gave once his mind to cards, his cards to tape,
An analyst's soul in a Boolean man –
Brainwashed by logic, his flow charts took shape.

And think this tape, all oxide shed away,
A pulse in the recording heads, I guess –
Gives somewhere back the bits it had been giv'n:
Alphanumeric data, yea and nay;
The random access mem'ry dataless –
The pow'r turned off in a programmer's heav'n.

Will had not only written poems until his death, he had enjoyed reciting them whenever he had a willing listener. As Dora was growing up, he recited poems to her at bedtime. When she married and was raising a family of her own, he continued his recitation at family events or at odd times. It is not surprising that Dora's children were influenced by Will's poetry. Dora appreciated Will's complex poems, but she also enjoyed the short, pithy ones. Her own poem about Will reveals this:

"There Was a Dad"

There was a dad
who had a daughter.
Swung her; spun her.
Chased her; caught her.
Hugged her; loved her.
Praised her; taught her.
Oh, what happiness
he brought her!

I, too, was influenced by Will's poetry. Following his death, I tried my hand at a sonnet. I wrote one that I addressed to Dora, which I included in *A Bouquet of Verse:*

How Do I See You?

How do I see you? Let me tell you how.
I see a babe whom God chose for me,
A wee developing personality.

I see you a child, cute dolls at your side.
When even-time comes, Dad's escort and guide:
"The owl and the pussycat went to sea,"
Soft bedtime crooning, your listening with glee.

A girl with music and horses to ride,
'Til time's swift stream changes you to a bride,
Later mother of sisters and brother.

I see you using God's gifts of teaching
And with compassion creating, reaching
Now teens, soon adults who will remember
You, but not as completely as I do.

I also was touched by Will's symbolic poems, in which he used metaphors to suggest the message of the poem, such as "Falling Leaves," which he wrote prior to his cancer and which ultimately predicted his death.

"Falling Leaves"

Ruddy red leaf,
What joy you show!
You welcome death as you
Gently float down
To a carpet of your
Brothers and sisters –
Carried on the wind,
Blessed by its loving breath –
A fond farewell to Life!

Sweep me gently, friend;
Pile me carefully, brother;
I have lived life free –
Kissed and caressed
By sun and smiling faces;
Loved and bathed
By rain-borne gentle tears,
And knowing that my brothers
Will be born anew in the coming spring.

At an early age, our granddaughter, Sara, began to love poetry. On the day that Will died, she wrote the following poem, in which she used repetition to enhance the message of her poem:

The Last Surrender

The world doesn't change at all;
The wind still blows, and a shrew scuttles to its nest below,
The ocean waves crash quite lowly and crumble
The stone so slowly.
No, the world doesn't change at all.

The hunger in my stomach scratches at me;
The homework in my head calls more faintly.
The German test my love has to take is still tonight.
The sun still sinks until she's out of sight.
The world doesn't change at all.

No storms smack branches on my window panes,
Though some shrew becomes prey, it is common place,
No ocean tides overcome the beach,
The stone does not tumble down in a giant piece.
No, the world doesn't change at all.

The lines that draw her face are as strong as can be.
The strength in herself, in her step keeps her steady.
The beside assistant never suited her right.
The thing she fears comes from a silent night.
The world doesn't change at all.

A teacher still writes down her lessons;
An athlete still goes to her training sessions;
A son gets off work and calls his mother;
A husband makes sure the trip is covered.
The world doesn't seem to change at all.

The man in the bed loved puns, puzzles, and rhymes.
The love by his side can tell it is time.
The world refuses to fall apart.
The world does not pause for a broken heart.

The world does not change
But the words are now wrong.

Wife turns to widow in the beat of a song.
Family links arms through satellite dishes;
Everyone sends love and good wishes.
The world does not change.
But we do.

Sara's poem became the last poem in my collection, *A Bouquet of Verse,* which I had printed and bound. I selected a picture of a bouquet of a variety of flowers for the cover. At Christmastime, I gave each family member a copy. It was my gift not only to each of them, but a tribute and a belated gift to Will.

Conclusion:

Now that my role has changed from nurse to widow, I look back on our marriage as complicated and interesting. Will had been such an intelligent, unique, and creative man that our lives were always eventful. Until he became increasingly ill and self-absorbed, we were good companions. We stayed together for fifty-seven years, sharing the 'ups and downs' of day-to-day living. Time changed our **love** for each other, but it still exists as a memory.

"How Did I Not Know?"
(To Will from Beth)

How did I not know until your breathing ceased
That I loved you so?

At first, I loved your wit,
your smile, your English ways,
your quick wink for me alone.
Then our natures grew and joined to make us one.
That was love, we knew.

How did we not know then that love is ever changing,
rearranging each of us?
That sorrow comes and sorrow goes
and sometimes joy replaces woes.

Did love yet remain when we grew old together?
Familiar habits, words and ways were second nature now —

a tiresome verse, a tale retold,
a body frail from being old.

How did I not know that when your breathing ceased,
your frame at last released
from misery and pain,
I would shout, "Not yet, Lord, not yet!"

But love thinks not of self alone,
The gift of memory remains.
So, I am here, and you are gone
to peace and joy forevermore,
For God is love, and love goes on.

THE END